Good Science
Student Workbook/Manual
Grades 4-6

DISTRIBUTED BY:
The Moore Foundation
P.O. Box 1
Camas, WA 98607

RICHARD B. BLISS, Ed.D. • JENNIFER M. ARENA, M.S.

Good Science for Home and Christian Schools Student Workbook/Manual

Book II: Grades 4-6

Copyright © 1993 Institute for Creation Research

All Rights Reserved

No part of this publication may be reproduced, stored in a retrieval system, or transmitted in any form or by any means—electronically, mechanically, by photocopying, recording, or otherwise—without prior permission of the Institute for Creation Research, with the exception of brief excerpts in magazine articles and/or reviews.

Dr. Richard B. Bliss and Jennifer M. Arena

Contributing Consultants:
Fred Willson, Home School Consultant (Science Education)
Steven Deckard, Ed.D. (Science Education)
Micky Seismore, Home School Parent (Biologist)
Janet Barnett, Elementary Teacher (K-6)
Monty Wyss, Principal (K-12)

Institute for Creation Research
P.O. Box 2667
El Cajon, CA 92021

Printed in the United States of America
ISBN #0-932766-29-3

Table of Contents

INTRODUCTION TO THE STUDENT MANUAL vi
ACKNOWLEDGMENTS vii

CHAPTER 1

LEVEL D: PHYSICAL SCIENCE
Relativity in God's Creation

- A. Relativity in God's Creation 11
- B. Locating Position Using a Reference Point in God's Creation 12
- C. Understanding Motion in God's Creation 14
- D. Polar Coordinates in God's Creation 16
- E. Coordinates that are Rectangular in God's Creation 18

CHAPTER 2

LEVEL D: LIFE SCIENCE
Environments in God's Creation

- A. Environments in God's Creation 21
- B. An Organism's Environment (Habitat) in God's Creation 23
- C. Environmental Changes in God's Creation 25
- D. Animals Respond to Their Environment in God's Creation 27
- E. Salinity for Organisms in God's Creation 28
- F. Plants and their Environment in God's Creation 30
- G. Total Environment in God's Creation 36
- H. Environmental Crossword Puzzle in God's Creation 38

CHAPTER 3

LEVEL E: PHYSICAL SCIENCE
Energy Sources in God's Creation

- A. Pre-Test for Energy Sources in God's Creation 43
- B. Review: Systems, Subsystems, and Variables in God's Creation 44
- C. Rolling Objects are Energy Sources in God's Creation 49
- D. Objects that Roll in God's Creation 51
- E. Paper Airplanes as Energy Sources in God's Creation 52
- F. Energy Transfer in God's Creation 54
- G. Energy Sources and Receivers in God's Creation 57
- H. Using Thermometers to Measure Evidence of Energy Interaction in God's Creation 59
-    Energy Sources and Plant Growth in God's Creation 61

I.	Temperature as Evidence of Energy Change in God's Creation	64
J.	Water Systems and Energy Flow in God's Creation	66
K.	Motion and Kinetic Energy in God's Creation	68

CHAPTER 4

LEVEL E: LIFE SCIENCE
Communities in God's Creation

A.	Communities in God's Creation	73
B.	Community Producers in God's Creation	75
C.	Do Plants Need Light to Grow in God's Creation?	78
D.	Experimenting Further with Plants in God's Creation	81
E.	The Terrarium in God's Creation	82
F.	Consumers in God's Creation	84
	Crossword Puzzle Fun in God's Creation	88
G.	Frogs in God's Creation	90
H.	Mealworms and Sow Bugs in God's Creation	92
I.	Decomposers in God's Creation	94
J.	Observing Yeast in God's Creation	96
K.	Summing up Communities in God's Creation	99

CHAPTER 5

LEVEL F: PHYSICAL SCIENCE
Electric and Magnetic Models in God's Creation

A.	Electric and Magnetic Models in God's Creation	103
B.	Electricity and Magnetism in God's Creation	105
C.	Examining Models for Energy Sources in God's Creation	108
D.	Working with Models in God's Creation	112
E.	A Model For a Magnetic Field in God's Creation	114
F.	Broken Magnet/Broken Relationship in God's Creation	118
G.	Seeing the Invisible become Visible in God's Creation	120

CHAPTER 6

LEVEL F: LIFE SCIENCE
Ecosystems in God's Creation

A.	Ecosystems in God's Creation	125
B.	Classroom Ecosystems in God's Creation	126
C.	Adding Crickets and Guppies to the Ecosystem in God's Creation	127
D.	Changes in the Aquarium and Terrarium Ecosystems in God's Creation	129

E.	Developing the Concept of an Ecosystem in God's Creation	131
F.	Investigating the Water Cycle in God's Creation	134
G.	Experimenting with BTB in God's Creation	137
H.	Investigating the Oxygen-Carbon Dioxide Cycle in God's Creation	140
I.	Cycles in an Ecosystem in God's Creation	146

INTRODUCTION TO THE STUDENT MANUAL

This student manual is written precisely in conjunction with the Good Science Teacher's Guide. It is designed to help the teacher with the inquiry phase of the "Good Science" curriculum. Teaching by the inquiry method generates questions and creative thought. Teachers often wonder about the kinds of questions they should be asking their pupils during experiments. The Good Science student guide is designed to help them with this. Nevertheless, we trust the teacher will use this only as a start, and then go much further with the student. There is so much more information available to the inquiring mind, it would be a tragedy to stop with these few questions, thus the teacher is encouraged to probe further as the opportunity arises.

At this point in time the student will be writing. It is very important that the instructor insist on the best writing practices. If a student feels that he/she can do sloppy writing in science or any other class outside of English, this will tend to become a habit. Also, careful reporting is important in the sciences and this should be stressed.

We have mentioned on several occasions in the teacher's guide that the amount of experimenting which can come from the Good Science approach is unlimited. If you have additional ideas for experiments, use them. Remember, always, that you cannot fail if you are stimulating a young mind to use the **process skills of scientific inquiry**. We are not as concerned with the correctness of the outcome at this point as we are with the level of critical thought that develops. The real **spirit of science** rests in: A **respect for logic**, a **longing for knowledge and understanding**, a **search for data and its meaning**, **considering the consequences**, **considering the premises**, and **questioning all things**. For you and me, who love the Lord as our Creator and Savior, all of this is done under the attributes of God. Can we hope for any less from our pupils?

ACKNOWLEDGMENTS

Even a workbook such as this requires many talents. The authors always get the headline credit, but it is so easy to forget those behind the scenes who really make it happen. We want to take this time to acknowledge the many individuals who were involved in this process. First and foremost of this group are the homeschool parents, Christian school teachers, and those professional science educators who were willing to give of their time to this project. These are the ones who gave their input during the Workshops and through the "Good Science" newsletter relating to the need of such a student manual as this. We listened to them, because they were on the front lines.

We also wish to acknowledge those who have the creative talent to lay out a workbook such as this. Neither of the authors has artistic or layout talents, so they must look to those who have. We can only remember the myriad of questions with which the authors were bombarded by the Desktop publisher, editors, and artists to get an accurate picture of the author's intent and purpose. Certainly they were a valuable critical factor in the makeup of this manual. Last of all, but by far the most important, we give credit to our Lord and Savior for inspiring us to produce such a curriculum for young people—a curriculum designed not only to reflect His attributes as Creator and Master Designer of all things, but also as our Savior and Lord!

The Authors

CHAPTER 1

LEVEL D: PHYSICAL SCIENCE

Relativity in God's Creation

An object may be standing still to an observer on Planet Earth, but it also could be moving at 1,000 miles per hour to an observer above the earth. We will use Mr. "O" (Mr. Observer) as a reference point throughout this relativity unit. We will be experimenting with this idea. Mr. "O" is observing the many facets of God's universe from several vantage points.

A. Relativity in God's Creation

1. What do you think **relative position** means? Explain in your own words.

   _____
   _____
   _____
   _____

2. What do you think **relative motion** is? Explain in your own words.

   _____
   _____
   _____
   _____

3. This is a challenge question: In your own words, can you explain what the word **"relativity"** means?

   _____
   _____
   _____

4. God is the Creator of all things, including **position**, **motion**, and **relativity**. What does this show you about the attributes of God?

   a. God has put everything together in an orderly fashion. _____

   b. _____

   c. _____

Mr. "O" is the observer in our **relativity unit**. He is often used as an external **reference point**.

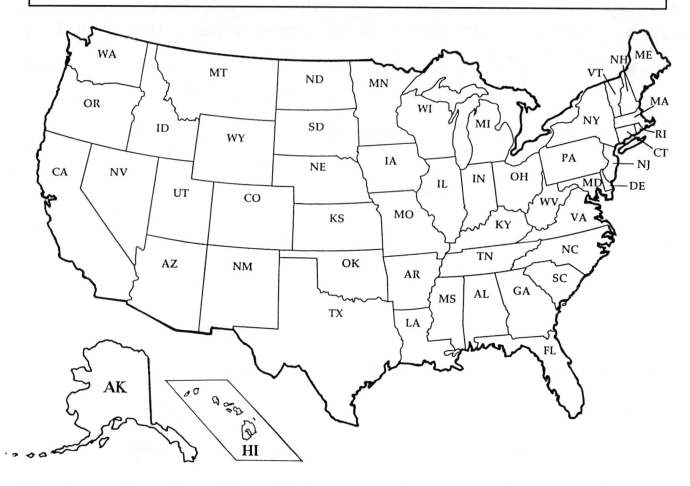

B. Locating Position Using a Reference Point in God's Creation

1. Mr. "O" lives in a state directly above the state of Alabama. What is the name of this state?

   _____

   _____

2. Can you pick two states that are directly below the state of Michigan?

   _____

3. Can you name a state that is directly to the right of the state of Idaho?

   _____

   _____

4. Can you name the state that is directly to the left of Colorado?

   _____

5. What is the **reference point** for locating each State in questions one through four?

   a. In Question 1 _____

   b. In Question 2 _____

   c. In Question 3 _____

   d. In Question 4 _____

6. The Bible is our **reference point** of truth. What does this show you about the attributes of God?

   a. God's Word is a **reference point** of truth to help us in this life.

   b. _____

   c. _____

Motion is a very important idea in science. Sometimes we are involved with moving objects and don't understand what is happening. Motion must have a reference point. What is the object moving in relation to? Try these experiments to start with. How many other experiments with motion can you find?

C. Understanding Motion in God's Creation

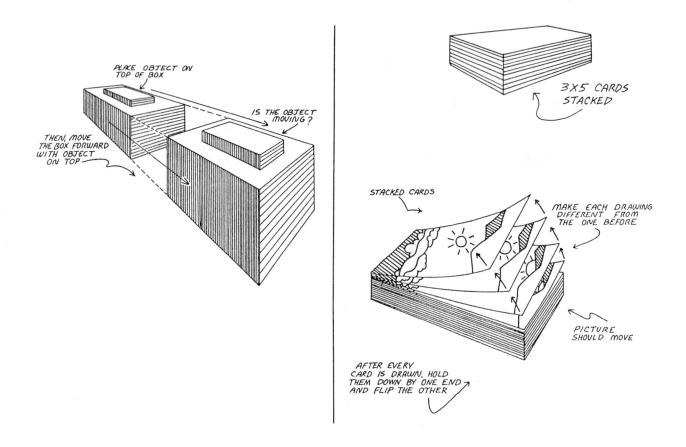

1. Look at the drawing and see if you can duplicate it with some objects around the house.

2. Move the object similar to the picture and state:

    a. Is the box moving? ❑ Yes ❑ No If so, what is it moving in relation to?

    _____

    b. Is the object on top of the box moving? ❑ Yes ❑ No If the answer is yes, what is it moving in relation to?

    _____

3. Try the same experiment with an object that has been placed on a movable chair.

    a. Is the object sitting in the chair moving? ❑ Yes ❑ No If the answer is yes, what is it moving in relation to?

    _____

    b. Is the chair moving? ❑ Yes ❑ No If the answer is yes, what is it moving in relation to?

    _____

4. Make a flip book similar to the one in drawing #2. Use about ten cards on which to make your drawings.

    a. Are the objects in the pictures moving? ❑ Yes ❑ No If the answer is yes, what are they moving in relation to?

    _____

    b. Look, in an encyclopedia or biology text, for information on the human eye and vision. After you have read this material, see if you can explain why pictures seem to move in your flip book.

    _____

    _____

    _____

    c. Explain why video and movies seem to move in such a normal way before our eyes. (You may wish to do some more reading about the eye.)

    _____

    _____

    _____

5. How does God fit into the idea of position and motion?

    a. God made a world for man to explore so He gave man the ability to recognize motion in that world.

    b. _____

    c. _____

Mr. "O," the observer, is used to help you understand "polar coordinates."

D. Polar Coordinates in God's Creation

1. How many **degrees** are there in the compass circle above? _____

2. How many **degrees** are there from Mr. "O's" left arm to his right arm? (Use the degree coordinates on the chart in the Appendix, if you wish.) _____

3. How many **degrees** are there from north to south? _____

4. How many **degrees** are there from Mr. "O's" left arm to his toes? (Use the degree coordinates on the chart in the Appendix, if you wish.) _____

5. Going clockwise, how many **degrees** are there from Mr. "O's" head to his right arm? _____

6. Describe the reference points used for:

   a. Question 2 _____

   b. Question 3 _____

   c. Question 4 _____

   d. Question 5 _____

7. God knows what is happening in every direction. What does this tell you about the attributes of God? (Psalm 103:12.)

   a. As far as the east is from the west and the north from the south, the Lord knows what is happening.

   b. _____

   c. _____

Both polar coordinates and rectangular coordinates need reference points. We will learn how this is true for rectangular coordinates in this unit.

E. Coordinates that are Rectangular in God's Creation

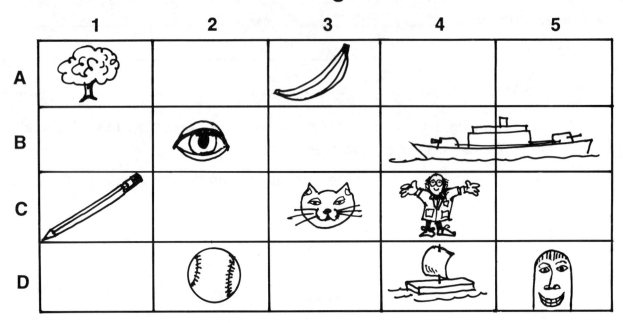

1. Using **rectangular coordinates**, find Mr. "O'" on the grid above. Give his coordinates (the "eye" is at B, 2). _____

2. Using **rectangular coordinates**, find the banana in the grid above. Give its coordinates. _____

3. Identify the object at coordinates D-2. _____

4. Using **rectangular coordinates**, locate the battleship. What are its coordinates? _____

5. God has given us a brain to be able to work out locations using **rectangular coordinates**. Animals can't do this. What does this show you about the attributes of God? (Romans 12:2-3.)

   a. God gave us a brain and senses to do complicated things.

   b. _____

   c. _____

CHAPTER 2

LEVEL D: LIFE SCIENCE

Environments in God's Creation

> Environments are always related to places where living systems can or cannot live. Environment is our new vocabulary word for this unit.

A. Environments in God's Creation

1. Write your own definition for the word "**environment**." What do you think it means?

   _____
   _____
   _____

2. Can you list some **environmental factors** that affect the life of an organism?

	Organism	Environmental Factor
1.		
2.		
3.		
4.		
5.		
6.		
7.		
8.		

3. Name three **environmental factors** on Planet Earth that make it possible for us to live on this planet.

   a. _____

   b. _____

   c. _____

4. God has created our planet with an **environment** that can sustain the kinds of life we see around us. What does this show you about the attributes of God?

   a. God designated the planet earth so that organisms could live on it.

   b. _____

   c. _____

> An organism's environment can also be its habitat. A habitat is a place where an organism lives.

B. An Organism's Environment (Habitat) in God's Creation

1. List the organisms in your terrarium habitat:

Organism	Environmental Factor
1.	
2.	
3.	
4.	
5.	
6.	
7.	

2. Determine the **population** of each of the organisms you listed in your terrarium. Write the number or amount of each beside the name of each organism above.

3. List five environmental factors that affect these organisms:

___

___

___

4. This is a challenge question: God created the perfect environment on Earth, but death and destruction entered the world due to the disobedience of Adam and Eve. What environmental factors were changed from His perfect creation?

___

___

___

5. Use the terms **population, organism,** and **habitat** to describe your terrarium environment.

   _____

   _____

   _____

6. What attribute of God fits this lesson?

   a. God changed things in man's habitat because he knew man had sinned and could no longer be depended upon to take care of his environment.

   b. _____

   c. _____

> Changes in environmental conditions can have a serious effect upon an organism. We will be studying these effects.

C. Environmental Outdoor Changes in God's Creation

1. Can you make some predictions about how you think changes in seasons will affect different organisms? List two environmental factors that change with the seasons of the year.

    a. Environmental Factor #1: _____

    b. Environmental Factor #2: _____

2. How do you think Environmental Factor #1 above will affect the organisms that live in the environment you are going to study? Fill in your predictions for each season of the year in the spaces below. Do the same thing for Environmental Factor #2.

Environmental Factor #1	Environmental Factor #2
Fall	**Fall**
Winter	**Winter**
Spring	**Spring**
Summer	**Summer**

3. A good scientist tests his predictions with actual observations. Fill in the following observation sheet based on your field trips. Make sure that you take good notes from your observations.

Date	Area Observed	Observation Notes

4. Do you think your predictions were correct? Circle those predictions in Question #2 that you found to be confirmed.

5. What can this lesson teach you about the attributes of God?

   a. God has created a world that is predictable even though it changes from season to season.

   b. _____

   c. _____

> When animals have an environmental choice, they will move to the environment that they like the best. These experiments will help you to understand this idea better.

D. Animals Respond to their Environment in God's Creation

1. Record the temperature on the hot end of the environment track. _____

2. Record the temperature on the cold end of the environment track. _____

3. Write a paragraph to explain what happened in this experiment (teachers manual II-15). What kind of environment do you think the organisms you tested prefer in nature?

   _____
   _____
   _____
   _____

4. God designed plants, animals, and people according to His plan and purpose. What does this tell you about the attributes of God?

   a. God has a plan and purpose for all organisms.

   b. _____

   c. _____

Aquatic animals, such as brine shrimp, have environmental preferences. From this experiment, you will notice how particular they can be.

E. Salinity for Organisms in God's Creation

1. What salt (NaCl) concentration is the best for brine shrimp?
   _____

2. Can you find the salt concentration that is not good for brine shrimp? What is that concentration?
   _____
   _____

3. Fill in the following bar graph and record the results of your brine shrimp-hatching experiment.

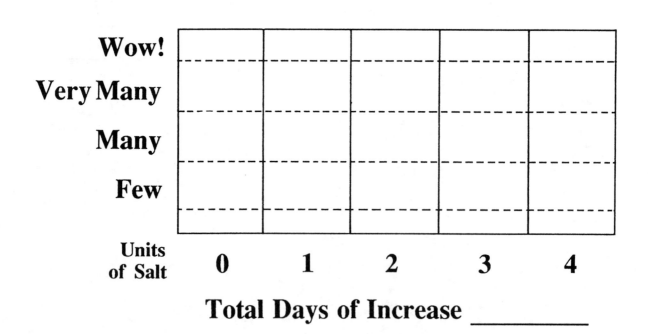

Data Sheet (bar graph) for _____

Wow!
Very Many
Many
Few

Units of Salt   0   1   2   3   4

Total Days of Increase _____

4. See if you can explain where the brine shrimp fit into the food chain or food web. Describe this in your own words.

   _____

   _____

   _____

   _____

5. Do you think you have discovered the **environmental conditions** necessary for brine shrimp to survive? What are they?

   _____

   _____

   _____

   _____

6. God shows us the spiritual condition that is necessary for us to continue serving Him. What does this show you about the attributes of God?

   a. God cares enough about me to send His son that I might survive with Him forever.

   b. _____

   c. _____

> Plants respond to **environmental factors** much like the way animals do. These experiments will help you to understand some of these factors.

F. Plants and their Environments in God's Creation

1. In your experiments with the different kinds of plants, you always used two of each type. Can you explain why it was important to have two of each type when you are conducting an experiment?

   _____
   _____
   _____

2. Use the charts on the following pages to record the results of your environmental experiments. The first two pages will help you to record the growth of plants in response to light and darkness. Use the last two pages for one of the other environmental factors you will be testing.

3. Can you make a prediction about what might happen in the light and dark environmental experiment?

   _____
   _____
   _____

4. Identify the **optimum range** of the following environmental factors for the plants which are listed:

   Light and darkness:

   bean _____

   grass _____

   clover _____

Temperature:

bean _____

grass _____

clover _____

Water:

bean _____

grass _____

clover _____

5. Can you think of an attribute of God that fits this experiment?

   a. God created and controls the environment in which we live.

   b. _____

   c. _____

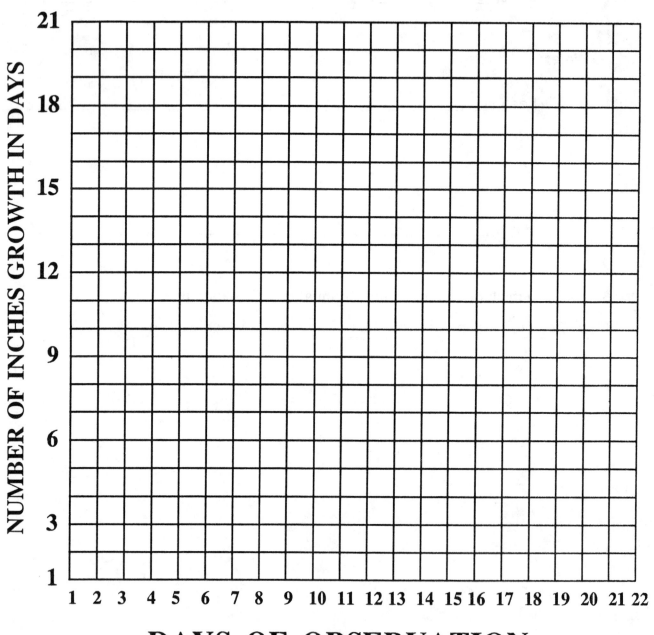

DATA CARD (BAR GRAPH) FOR: SET PLACED IN SUFFICIENT LIGHT

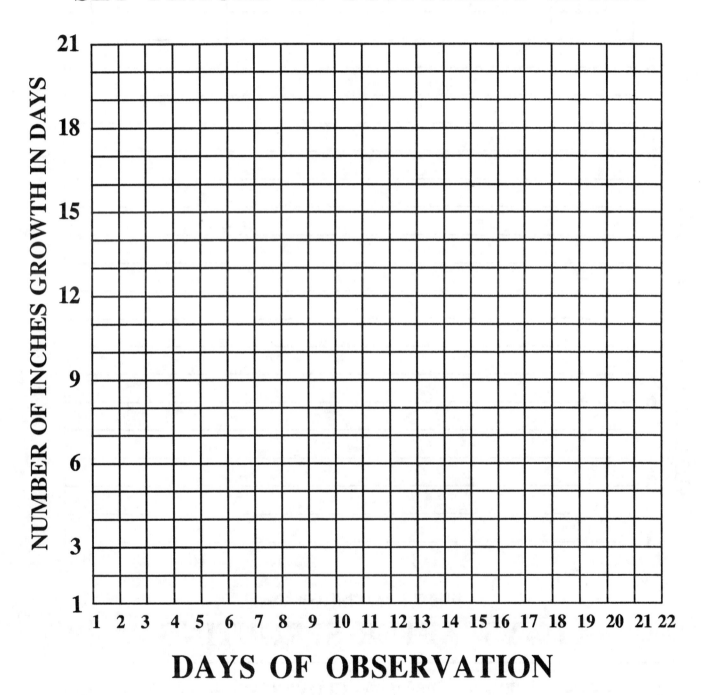

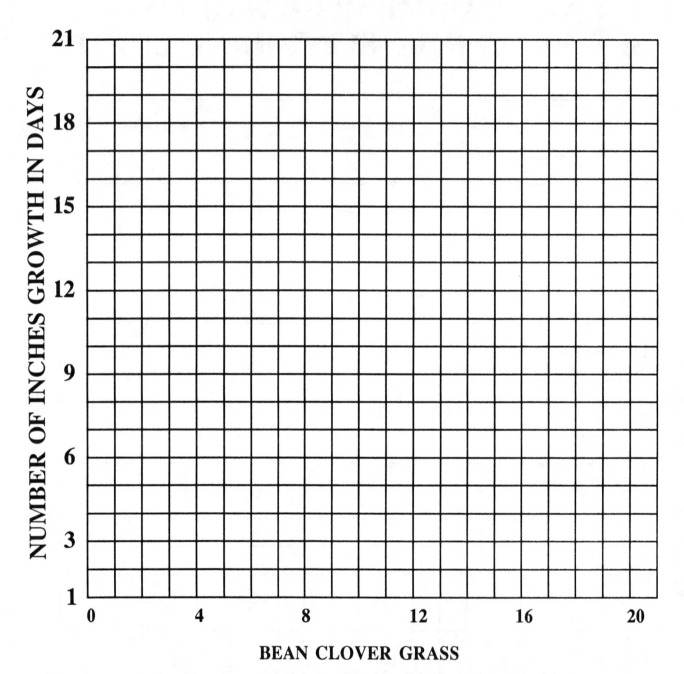

DATA CARD (BAR GRAPH) FOR: EXPERIMENTAL GROUP

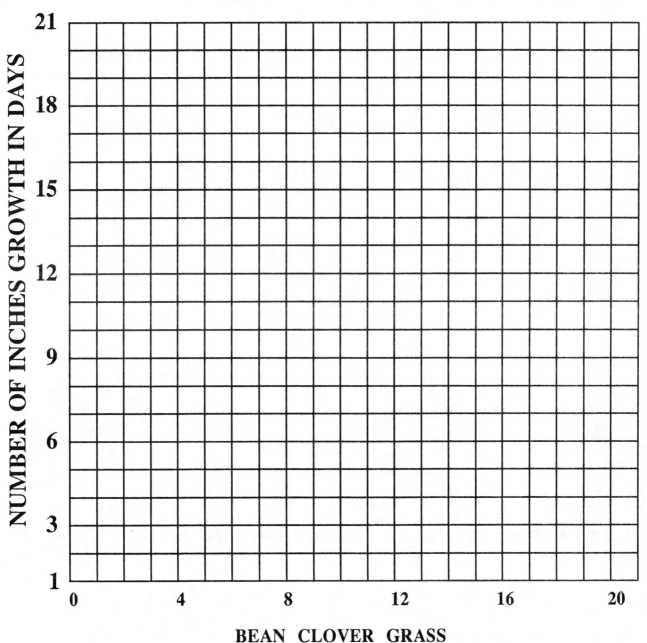

> You will be working with a total environmental plan during these experiments. Make careful observations of your terrarium.

G. Total Environment in God's Creation

1. Use the data you collected from your environment experiments with plants and animals to make a terrarium. Your plan should include as many environmental factors as possible. State below which organisms you will place in your terrarium, and which environment is most suitable.

	Organism	Most Suitable Environment
1.		
2.		
3.		
4.		
5.		
6.		
7.		
8.		
9.		
10.		

2. Draw a picture of your terrarium in the space below. Label the contents of the terrarium.

3. God created many different environments on Planet Earth which can support many different kinds of plants and animals. What does this show you about the attributes of God?

   a. God has a total environmental plan.

   b. _____

   c. _____

The following unit will give you a chance to become more familiar with organisms and environmental factors.

H. Environmental Crossword Puzzle in God's Creation

38

ACROSS

1. God created these on the third day of creation.
5. You can find these in a zoo.
10. A nickname for a doctor who takes care of animals.
11. What does Jesus want us to open in Revelation 3:20?
12. The life cycle of many animals begins with an ___.
14. The last stage in a life cycle.
17. A French word for "the."
19. The abbreviation for air conditioner.
20. "Joy ____ the World." Fill in the missing word.
22. The first stage in any life cycle.
24. A big animal that eats grass.
25. Abbreviation for Evolution Theory.
27. For people, we count growth by every _____.
28. A very important thing to have in the growth cycle.
29. Noah and his family survived the ____.

DOWN

2. This includes birth, growth, and death.
3. The abbreviation for television.
4. The birth cycle of a plant starts with this.
6. What should you say when someone wants you to do something that you know you shouldn't do?
7. A meal worm has one birth stage—an egg, and three growth stages: larvae, pupae, and ____.
8. An Old Testament word that means "not" (Hosea 1:5).
9. When living things decay in the death cycle, where do they go? Into the ____, where they help new life to grow.
13. What will you continue to do until you become an adult?
15. An organism in its earliest stages of development.
16. Something that is round on a bicycle.
18. This is what you need to do to grow.
21. A monocotyledon has how many parts?
23. When you cut one seed into two pieces, each piece becomes a ____.
26. A dicotyledon has how many halves?

**Choose from the list of words below
to answer the questions for this crossword puzzle.**

a.c.	door	food	no	to
adult	eat	grow	one	t.v.
animals	egg	half	plants	two
birth	embryo	life cycle	seed	vet
cow	e.t.	le	soil	year
death	flood	lo	tire	

CHAPTER 3

LEVEL E: PHYSICAL SCIENCE

Energy Sources in God's Creation

> This pre-test is designed to see what you remember about energy sources. You will be reviewing both potential and kinetic energy.

A. Pre-Test for Energy Sources in God's Creation

1. Write all you can remember about **energy sources**. Include everything you know about where energy comes from.

   _____
   _____
   _____

2. Write everything you can think of about **potential energy**.

   _____
   _____
   _____

3. Write everything you can think of about **kinetic energy**.

   _____
   _____
   _____

4. God created all energy. What does this show you about the attributes of God?

   a. God is the real source of all energy.

   b. _____

   c. _____

This will be a review of ideas and terms that are very important in science. **Systems, subsystems, and variables** are key terms used in science.

B. Review: Systems, Subsystems, and Variables in God's Creation

1. Follow system "P" as it goes through some changes, and answer the questions below each drawing. The drawings below are for your review.

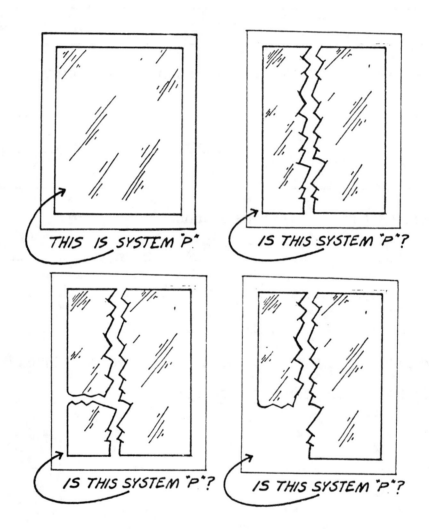

2. Construct a battery and bulb like the drawing below:

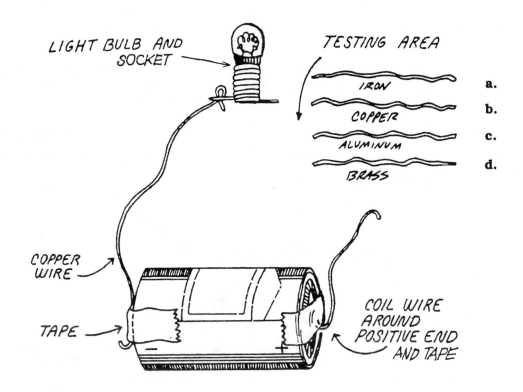

3. After you construct your battery-and-bulb **system**, state how many **subsystems** there are in the system. _____

4. Connect your battery-and-bulb-testing **system** to each piece of wire listed. Why are these called variables?

   _____

   _____

   _____

5. How many **variables** are there? _____

6. What effect did each **variable** have on the battery-and-bulb **system**?

   a. _____

   b. _____

   c. _____

   d. _____

7. When you did this experiment, what evidence of interaction did you observe?

   _____
   _____
   _____
   _____

8. Using a BTB solution in a plastic container similar to the one in the drawing below, see if you can answer the questions about this experiment. (Follow the instructions in the Teacher's Guide.)

   ADD VINEGAR DROP BY DROP
   VINEGAR
   THE SOLUTION SHOULD START TO TURN YELLOW
   ADD WATER DROP BY DROP
   A

   WATER
   FILL ABOUT 3/4 WATER AND BTB SOLUTION
   B

   a. How many subsystems can you count in the BTB system? _____

   b. Which subsystem showed evidence of interaction when something was added?

   _____

   c. Give your best idea as to why this subsystem showed evidence of interaction?

   _____
   _____
   _____

9. Bring the spinning system in that you used in Book I. An example of this system is in the drawing below.

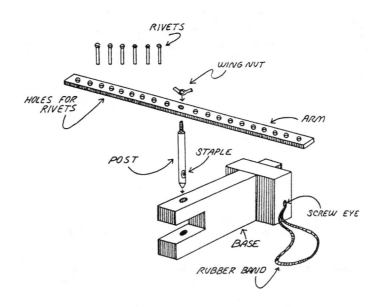

a. Count the number of **subsystems** that you can find in the spinning **system** and state them here. _____

_____

b. After making three turns on your spinning system with **one rivet** at each end, count the number of turns that you observed? Make three tries, and calculate the **average**. _____

c. After making three turns on your spinning **system** with **two rivets** on each end, record the number of turns that you observed. Make three tries, and calculate the **average**. _____

d. After making three turns on your spinning **system** with **three rivets** on each end, record the **average** number of turns that you observed? _____

e. What was the **variable** in your experiments with the spinning **system**?

_____

_____

_____

47

f. Make a **histogram** from all the scientific data that you have collected so far.

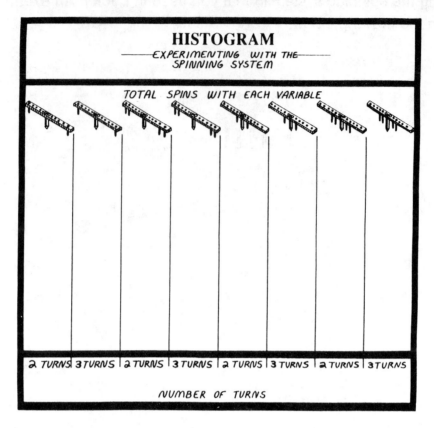

10. God has created a complicated and very precise universe. What does this say about the attributes of God?

    a. God is not a variable. He is the same yesterday, today, and forever.

    b. _____

    c. _____

Sometimes we forget that energy sources are objects that can make things happen. In science, when energy makes things happen, this is called *work*. We are going to use rolling objects to help you understand this idea better.

C. Rolling Objects are Energy Sources in God's Creation

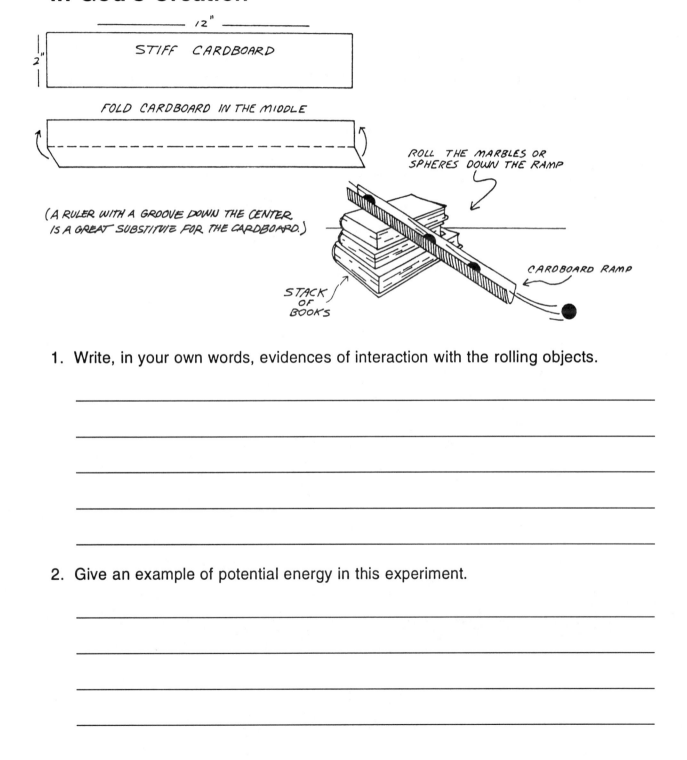

1. Write, in your own words, evidences of interaction with the rolling objects.

   _____
   _____
   _____
   _____
   _____

2. Give an example of potential energy in this experiment.

   _____
   _____
   _____
   _____

3. Can you give one example of kinetic energy that you observed in this experiment?

_____

_____

_____

_____

4. We all have the potential to be followers of Christ, but we need to act (kinetic energy) with faith to do the will of God (Hebrews 12:1,2). What does this tell you about the attributes of God?

   a. God wants us to trust Him and serve Him with all of our energy.

   b. _____

   c. _____

> More experiments with objects that roll. Objects that roll can show evidence of interaction in many ways. Carbon paper will help in this experiment.

D. Objects that Roll in God's Creation

1. Name some variables that made the tracks you observed different.

   _____
   _____
   _____

2. Use our vocabulary word, *inferences*. What **inferences** can you make about the mystery tracks you observed?

   _____
   _____
   _____
   _____

3. God provides a uniform world in which we live. This gives us an opportunity to explore the variables in His creation. Does this show something about the attributes of God?

   a. God wants us to understand Him through His creation.

   b. _____

   c. _____

There are many kinds of energy sources. These experiments with paper airplanes will help you to understand some of them.

E. Paper Airplanes as Energy Sources in God's Creation

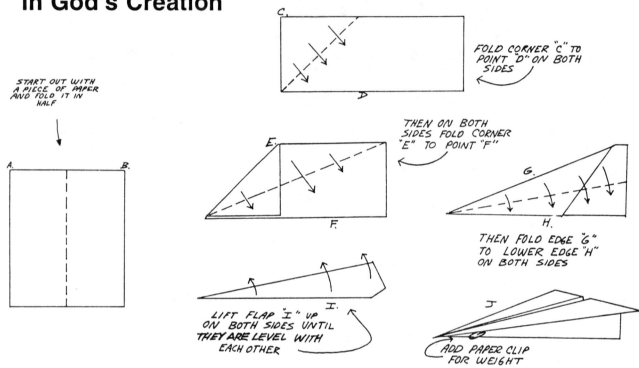

1. Make your own paper airplane. You can use the model above, if you like. Now fly your airplane. **After you have practiced with three turns, you can start to make your flights official.** You can take the best of three flights.

2. After you have made three official flights, record the distance of each below:

    a. _____

    b. _____

    c. _____

3. What **variables** do you think affected your flight distance?

    a. _____

    b. _____

    c. _____

4. Of all the variables you mentioned in Question 3, circle the ones you have control over.

5. What improvements could you make in your airplane design that would make it go farther?

   _____

   _____

   _____

6. God has control over all the variables in this world. What does this show you about the attributes of God?

   a. God is not a variable in our life, but our reaction to Him varies, based on our desire to love and obey Him.

   b. _____

   c. _____

> Energy can be transferred from one object to another. These experiments will help you to understand how this happens. You will be using the term potential energy in these experiments.

F. Energy Transfer in God's Creation

1. In your own words, state what the word energy means.

   _____

   _____

2. Can you identify the **energy source**, the **energy transfer**, and the **new energy source**?

   1. _____   2. _____   3. _____

3. What was the energy receiver in the pictures above? State what each could be called in a, b, and c.

   (a) _____

   (b) _____

   (c) _____

4. Tell what *potential energy* is, in your own words.

   _____

   _____

5. Name any object in the room that you think has **potential energy**. Explain why it has potential energy.

_____

_____

_____

6. Label the drawings in the energy chain below using the terms "potential" and "kinetic" energy; energy "source" and energy "receiver:"

LIGHTED MATCH

1. _____

2. _____

START FIRE

2. _____

FIRE

3. _____

COOKING POT

4. _____

HUNGRY MAN

5. _____

55

7. What does this lesson show you about the attributes of God?

   a. Sometimes God waits (with potential energy), and sometimes God acts (with kinetic energy).

   b. _____

   c. _____

These experiments will help you to understand more about **energy sources** and **energy receivers**. You also will become acquainted with **energy chains**.

G. Energy Sources and Receivers in God's Creation

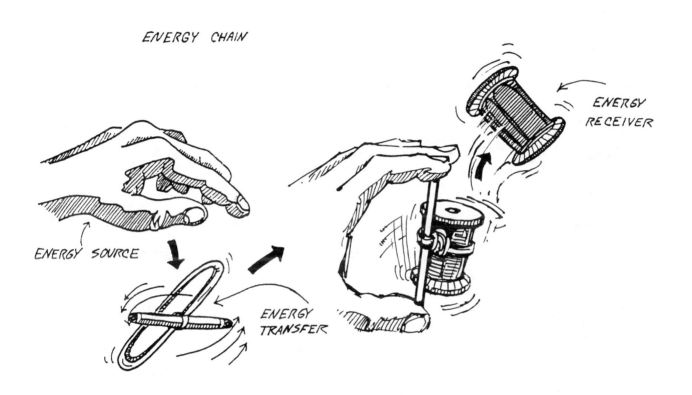

1. How many objects are there in this energy system? _____

2. What **energy source** is transferring energy into the "spool" system?

   _____

3. What is the **energy receiver** in this "spool" system?

   _____

4. What evidences of energy transfer are shown in the "spool" system?

   _____

   _____

5. Describe the energy transfer when the rubber band around the crayon is released.

   _____

   _____

   _____

6. Describe an **energy chain** in your own words.

   _____

   _____

   _____

7. Can you think of two other **energy chains** in this experiment?

   _____

8. How can you relate this experience with **energy sources** to our God of creation?

   a. God uses us to do His work on earth. We become a spiritual energy chain for others.

   b. _____

   c. _____

> Thermometers help us see the evidence of energy interaction with objects.

H. Using Thermometers to Measure Evidence of Energy Interaction in God's Creation

1. Measure the temperature of four objects in your room. List the temperatures of these objects below:

Object	Temperature

2. Experimenting with temperature, measure the temperature of a cup of hot water and a cup of cold water. Combine the two cups and measure the temperature of the mixture. Record your results below:

Hot water _____ Cold water _____ Mixture _____

3. Try the experiment in Number 2 again. This time, change one **variable** such as length of time, type of container, temperature of hot or cold water, etc. Try to predict what the temperature mixture might be. Don't forget to write your prediction before you take the temperature of the mixture. Record your results in the following chart:

Temperature of Hot Water	Temperature of Cold Water	Variable	Prediction	Actual Temperature of Mixture

4. Write all you can about what you learned from this experiment.

_____

_____

_____

_____

5. Sometimes we are tempted to do the wrong thing, but God is faithful, and He won't allow us to be tempted beyond our ability. God even makes a way for us to escape from temptation if we so choose (I Corinthians 10:13). What does this show you about the attributes of God?

   a. God can predict the variables in your life that will be a challenge to your faith, and He provides for them.

   b. _____

   c. _____

> This is a special experiment that does not appear in the teacher's manual. This experiment appeared in the Good Science Newsletter, Fall, Vol. 3, No. 3. The experiment emphasized energy.

Energy Sources and Plant Growth in God's Creation

1. Objectives: The pupil will be able to:
    a. understand how the sun is a source of both heat and light energy;
    b. observe and be able to construct a solar heater;
    c. understand the nature of a control in an experiment;
    d. make a hypothesis about the size of the pan and the amount of heat collected;
    e. state an attribute of God that relates to this experiment.

2. Materials
    - 4 measuring cups
    - 2 large aluminum pie tins (painted black)
    - 2 small aluminum pie tins (painted black)
    - 4 thermometers
    - wax paper (or plastic wrap)
    - tap water
    - direct sunlight

3. Guidelines for the Teacher
    This experiment is not only interesting and practical, it also tells much about the energy of the sun in God's creation. You might wish to question the pupil on what would happen if the sun were closer to us. What would happen if it were farther away? These questions will lead to the attribute of God concerning His creative genius.

    From a scientific experiment point of view, we will be using a control group where nothing changes, and an experimental group where only the size of the dish changes. Emphasize to the student that all true experiments in science have a controlled and an experimental side to them. You might wish to take time to emphasize the importance of this approach. The purpose of the experiment is to determine how this energy might be used by living things. How important is this energy to a plant, as well as to us?

4. Activities

   a. Collect the four measuring cups and label them as follows:

   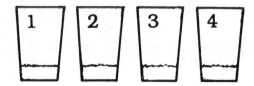

   b. Fill each cup with 100 ml. of water, enough to barely cover the bottom. You may use ounces (3.25) or ml. (100), but whichever you use, there must be exactly the same amount of water in each cup.

   c. Take the temperature of each cup of water with your thermometers. Keep the thermometers in the water for at least two minutes.

   d. Record the temperatures in each of the cups using their own thermometers. For example:

   e. Pour the water from each cup into the black-painted pie pans. Make sure that each cup and its pie pan has the same label. Cup one (1) water goes into cup one (1) pie tin, cup two (2) water goes into cup two (2) pie tin, etc.

   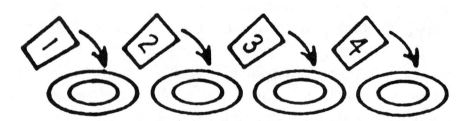

f. Cover the plates with wax or plastic wrap and set in direct sunlight for 20 minutes.

g. After 20 minutes, pour the water from the pie tins back into the cups.

h. Using the same thermometers you used for each cup, measure the temperature change and record it on your chart.

i. Make a bar graph to show your results (see example).

j. Repeat the experiment and record the results on the same bar graph. (How will you change your bar graph to do this?)

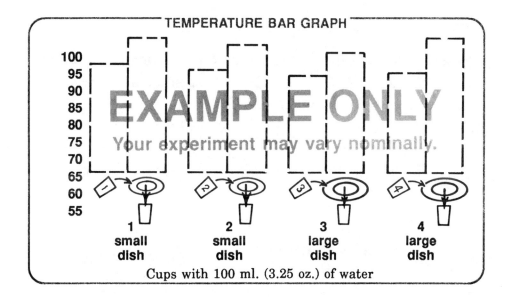

k. State, in your own words, what this experiment has to do with growing plants:

_____

_____

_____

63

Temperature is a means for detecting evidence of energy interaction. We can measure changes that occur from energy sources by watching temperature changes.

I. Temperature as Evidence of Energy Change in God's Creation

1. Measure the temperature of a container of cold water and record your results below.

   _____

   _____

2. What happens to the temperature of the water when you heat the container? Heat the container for three (3) minutes and then measure the temperature again. What is the new temperature?

   _____

3. What was the energy source you used to heat the water?

   _____

4. How can you tell that there was an energy transfer?

   _____

   _____

5. What was the temperature change that caused the energy transfer to the container of cold water?

   _____

   _____

6. Could the hot water be considered an energy source? Explain this in your own words.

   _____

   _____

   _____

7. Try an experiment that will transfer the energy of the hot water to another container of cold water. Check the temperature of the cold water before and after you add the hot water, and record it below.

Temperature Before: _____ **Temperature After:** _____

8. What was the evidence of energy transfer in your experiment? _____
_____

9. How much temperature change (in degrees Celsius or Fahrenheit) was caused by this energy transfer? _____
_____

10. The gift of the Holy Spirit is the energy source from God that gives us the power to live as Jesus commanded. What does this show you about the attributes of God?

    a. God gives us the energy to be an effective witness for Him.

    b. _____

    c. _____

> These experiments will help you to understand more about **energy systems**, by observing **energy flow**.

J. Water Systems and Energy Flow in God's Creation

1. List the variables in the hot and cold water experiment.

   _____

   _____

   _____

2. Graph your measurements for the temperature of the cold and hot water on the chart below:

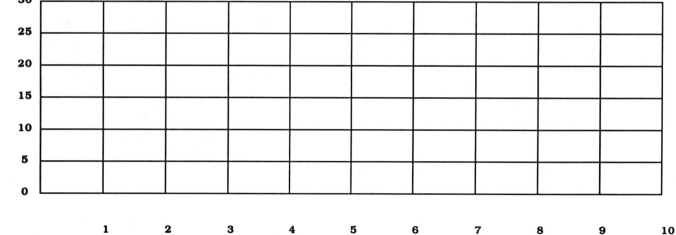

3. What did you observe after ten (10) minutes?

   _____

   _____

   _____

4. Write a paragraph to explain, in your own words, what the graph shows.

   _____

   _____

   _____

   _____

5. Friendships are like energy transfers because people "rub off" on each other. In order for us to stay on fire for God, we need to go back to the energy source, which involves spending time with God and His Word. What does this show you about the attributes of God?

   a. God is the only ultimate source of spiritual energy.

   b. _____

   c. _____

67

These experiments will deal with **motion as evidence for kinetic energy.**

K. Motion and Kinetic Energy in God's Creation

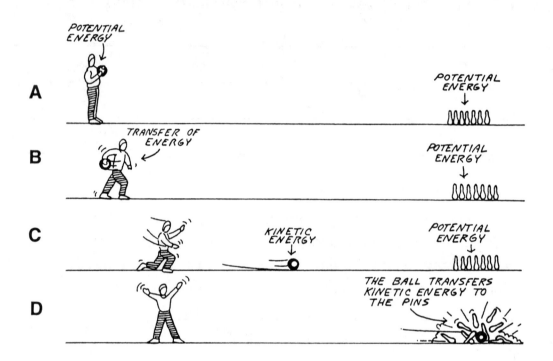

1. Can you think of some variables that would affect the results shown in "D"?
   _____
   _____

2. What object in the pictures above is both an energy receiver and an energy source?
   _____

3. Explain, in your own words, how an object can be both an energy receiver and an energy source?
   _____
   _____
   _____

4. What were the variables in your experiment with kinetic energy and motion?

_____

_____

_____

5. What were the energy sources and the energy receivers in your experiment?

_____

_____

_____

6. Describe what you think might be an energy chain.

_____

_____

_____

7. One variable that affects our movement toward a close relationship with God has to do with obedience. What does this tell you about the attributes of God?

   a. God is like a father; He wants us to obey Him.

   b. _____

   c. _____

CHAPTER 4

LEVEL E: LIFE SCIENCE

Communities in God's Creation

This series of observations will help you understand the whole idea of **communities** better.

A. Communities in God's Creation

1. Explain, in your own words, what you think a **community** is.

   _____

   _____

   _____

   _____

2. Find a picture in a magazine that represents the same kind of **natural community** that you live in now. Paste the picture in the box below.

3. Use a camera to take a picture of **two different communities**. (You might want to take a field trip to the zoo, park, river, or lake.) Paste your pictures in the space below.

4. God knows that many different kinds of plants and animals work together in a natural community. God also created different types of people so that they might work together. What does this show about the attributes of God?

   a. God wants me to learn to work with other people.

   b. _____

   c. _____

In this section you will learn more about **producers** in a **plant community**.

B. Community Producers in God's Creation

1. Draw, as best you can, the seed parts of a **living monocotyledon** and a **living dicotyledon**.

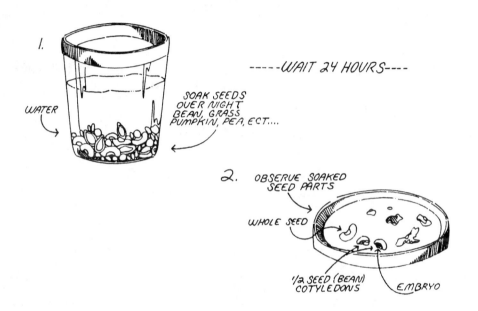

2. Explain, in your own words, what you think the **embryo** does.

   _____

   _____

   _____

3. What do you think **cotyledons** do?

   _____

   _____

   _____

4. Which parts of the seed did not grow?

   _____

   _____

   _____

5. Which parts did grow?

   _____

   _____

   _____

6. Record the growth of the different seed parts on the following graph.

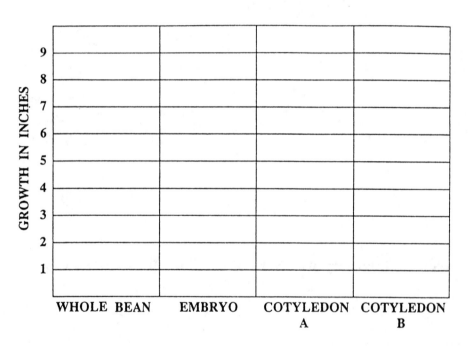

DATA GRAPH FOR SEED PARTS GROWTH

7. Which seeds were able to grow in water alone?

   _____

   _____

   _____

8. Which seeds were able to grow on a wet paper towel?

   _____

   _____

   _____

9. Can you think of three (3) places a seed might not be able to grow?

   a. _____

   b. _____

   c. _____

10. The parable of the seed and the sower compares the growth of Christians to the growth of seeds (Matthew 13:3-9,18-23). How does this show you something about the attributes of God?

    a. God wants us to grow into strong followers of Christ.

    b. _____

    c. _____

> These are experiments that will help you to understand more about the very important **plant producers**. Read the experiment in the text on Page IV-9.

C. Do Plants Need Light to Grow in God's Creation?

1. Why did you use a **control group** of plants in this experiment?

   _____
   _____
   _____
   _____

2. Can you list the variables you used with the **experimental group(s)** of plants?

   _____
   _____
   _____
   _____

3. What did you observe about the plants that grew in the dark?

   _____
   _____
   _____
   _____

4. Complete the following data graph for your experiment. Record your control group and **experimental group** separately.

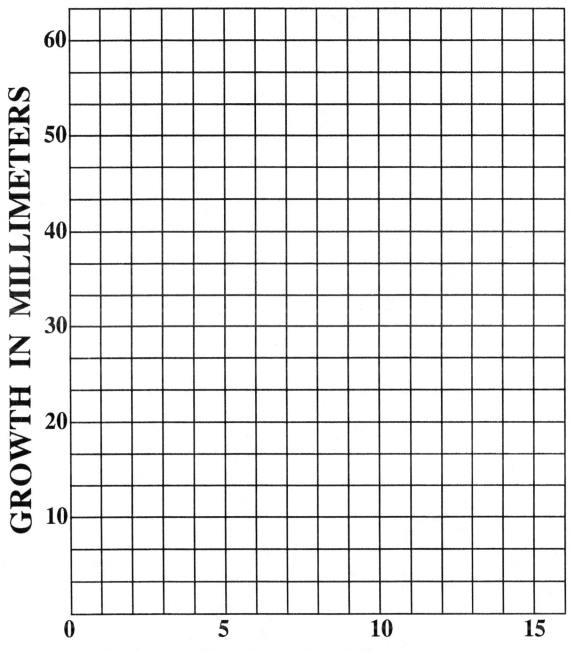

5. God has called you out of the darkness to live as a child of light (Ephesians 5:8), because He wants you to grow strong in Christ. What does this show you about the attributes of God?

   a. God wants us to cast our light as an example to others.

   b. _____

   c. _____

This section will help you to learn much more about plants and plant communities by measuring their growth under certain conditions.

D. Experimenting Further with Plants in God's Creation

1. Let's do some measurements to see what happens to bean plants if we remove the **cotyledons** at different times in the growth cycle. Fill in the data graph below as your experiment progresses.

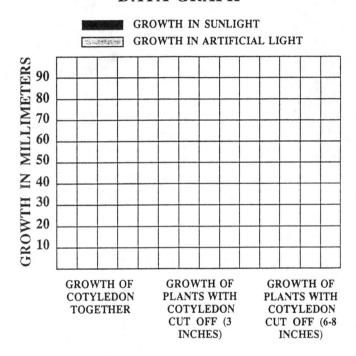

2. Are the **cotyledons** useful to the developing bean plant? How are they useful? Explain this in your own words.

   _____

   _____

   _____

3. God has created everything for a reason, even though we don't always understand those reasons. What does this show you about the attributes of God?

   a. God has a purpose for me.

   b. _____

   c. _____

81

> The terrarium will be your main point for observation. This is your chance to watch different organisms of your choice up close.

E. The Terrarium in God's Creation

1. Set up a terrarium with your favorite organisms. Label the organisms you chose for your terrarium. Place the labels outside the terrarium.

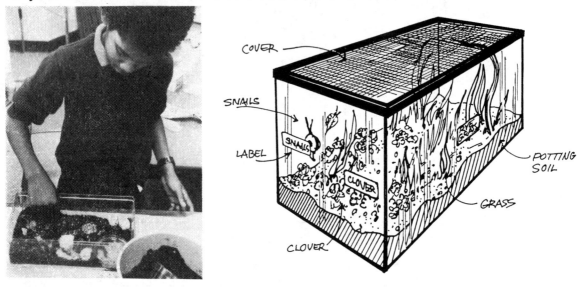

2. Draw your favorite terrarium organism in the space below and name it.

3. List several facts about the organisms in your terrarium.

_____
_____
_____

4. God cares for all of the little animals in your terrarium, so He has provided for them by designing them in special ways and by making food for them to eat. What does this show you about the attributes of God?

   a. God cares about the smallest things.

   b. _____

   c. _____

> This section will be used to study important **consumers** in God's creation.

F. Consumers in God's Creation

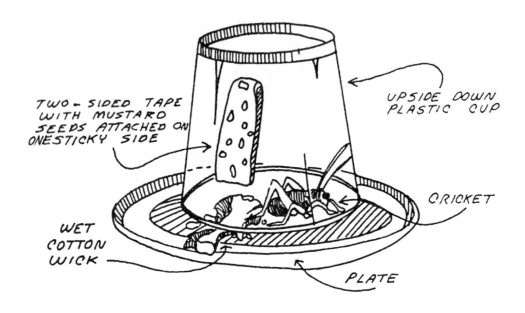

1. In your own words, explain the difference between a **consumer** and a producer.

   _____
   _____
   _____
   _____

2. Set up a cricket **consumer** chamber experiment like the one above. Place your seeds in the chamber and make daily observations on the chart below. What are your conclusions?

   _____
   _____
   _____

DATA CHART FOR _____

DAYS	SEEDS IN CHAMBER	SEEDS EATEN

TIME OF DAY OR NIGHT

KINDS OF SEEDS

SEEDS LEFT OVER EACH DAY

3. In the space next to its name in Question 2 above, tell what each **consumer** eats.

4. Fill in the following data chart as you observe your terrarium over time.

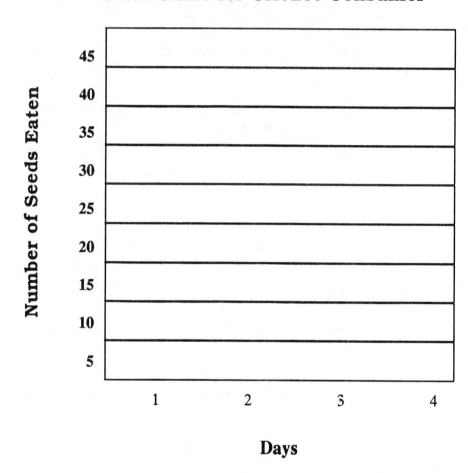

Data Chart for Cricket Consumer

5. See if you can find the food chain relationship between the organisms in the terrarium. Say something about this in the space below.

_____
_____
_____
_____

6. Now see how long your food chain gets. Use the blank spaces below to fill in the specific organisms from your terrarium.

_____ eaten by _____ which is
   (producer)

eaten by _____ which is eaten by _____

which is eaten by _____

7. God is the One who created the giant terrarium called Earth and all of the **producers** and **consumers** in it. What does this show you about the attributes of God?

   a. God planned the earth from its very inception. According to Scripture, everything was made by God. This is His creation.

   b. _____

   c. _____

87

The following material will make you better acquainted with consumers and producers in a fun way.

Crossword Puzzle Fun in God's Creation

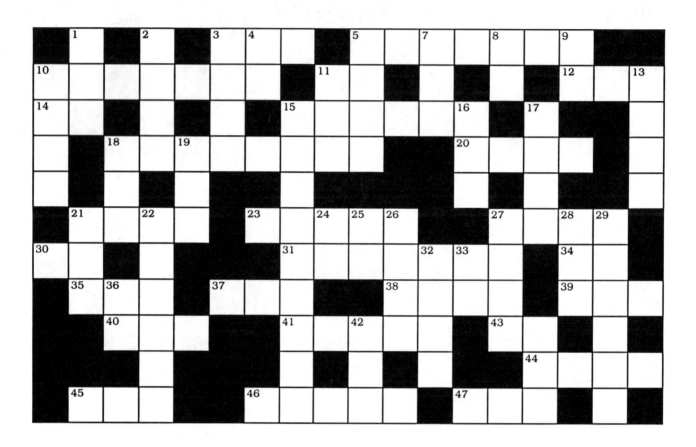

**Choose from the list of words below
to answer the questions for this crossword puzzle.**

go	Ed	worm	Sr.	home	cares
embryo	worship	ask	born	or	Spirit
RNA	organism	grow	Hi	zoo	u. e.
rat	egg	habitat	man	created	liar
web	oil	one	ants	life cycle	gas
larvae	at	Jesus	test	Me	e. t.
bat	dry	safe	feta	sew	hay

88

ACROSS

3. A boy grows up to be one of these.
5. "Come, let us ___ and bow down: let us kneel before the LORD our maker" (Psalm 95:6).
10. The place where an animal lives.
11. What cars do at a green light.
12. "___, and it shall be given unto you; seek, and ye shall find . . ." (Matthew 7:7).
14. Sounds like oar.
15. The stage of many insects' life cycles that comes after the egg stage.
18. Another name for a plant or an animal.
20. What happens to plants if they get water and sunlight.
21. The first stage of the life cycle of a plant.
23. Who paid the price for your sins?
27. Hard-working little insects.
30. The King James Version of the Bible sometimes uses this word for "you."
31. God ___ the world in six days, and on the seventh day He rested.
34. Abbreviation for a word processor.
35. A spider's home.
37. What do horses and cows eat?
38. A type of cheese used in Greek recipes.
39. In Mark 6:13, the disciples put ___ on many sick people, and healed them.
40. The opposite of wet.
41. Why do some people not believe the Word of God? Jesus gives the answer as He explains the parable of the sower in Luke 8:14. He says that they "are choked with ___ and riches and pleasures of this life. . . ."
43. ___, myself, and I.
44. What do plants grow in?
45. A place where you find many animals.
46. The final stage of any life cycle.
47. An animal that comes out at night and uses radar to find its way around.

DOWN

1. Something from the kitchen that you can use to catch bugs.
2. "A poor man is better than a ___" (Proverbs 19:22).,
3. Another name for mom.
4. "Behold, I stand ___ the door and knock: if any man hear my voice and open the door, I will come in to him" (Revelation 3:10).
5. The early bird get the ___.
7. Abbreviation for Ribonucleic Acid.
8. Another word for hello.
9. Another word for papa.
10. Where you live.
11. Fuel for a car.
13. The bride and groom do this at a wedding.
15. A name for all of the stages of an organism (two words).
16. The first stage of an insect.
17. Your birthday celebrates the day you were ___.
18. How many divisions are in a monocotyledon seed?
19. Who is our Father in Heaven?
21. What does a sewing machine do?
22. The growth part of a seed.
24. Abbreviation for senior.
25. The last two letters in "true."
26. If you are not in danger, then you are ___.
27. God created ___ on the sixth day of creation.
28. How many divisions are in a dicotyledon seed?
29. God is actually three in one: God the Father, God the Son, and God the ___.
32. Another word for exam.
33. What are the fifth and twentieth letters of the alphabet?
36. A guy's name.
42. A long-tailed animal larger than a mouse.

> **The frog is the focus in our study of the food pyramid.** We will learn much about him and his relationship to other organisms.

G. Frogs in God's Creation

1. Make a **food pyramid** for the organisms in your terrarium.

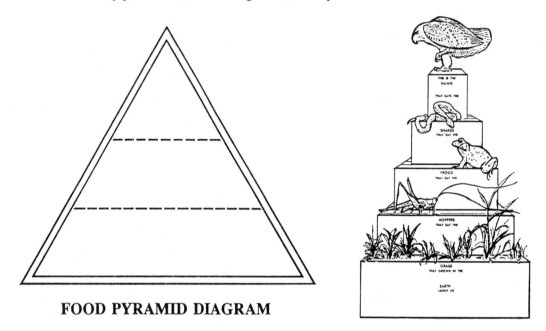

FOOD PYRAMID DIAGRAM

2. What organisms would you place above the frog in a different food pyramid? Explain.

   _____
   _____
   _____
   _____

3. Examine your frog carefully. Based on your observations, can you explain how the following parts of your frog are specially designed? What does each part do?

   Legs _____

   Tongue _____

   Throat _____

Mouth _____

Skin _____

Eyes _____

4. Just as with the frog, we can see God's hand in the many things He designed for specific purposes. God also created you for a specific reason. What does this show you about the attributes of God?

   a. He had a plan and purpose for me. God cares for me.

   b. _____

   c. _____

This section will give you an opportunity to do some experimenting and also to raise some of your own organisms. Don't feel that the organisms suggested are the only organisms that will work in your study. Try some others, as well.

H. Mealworms and Sow Bugs in God's Creation

1. Using a magnifying lens, see how many different characteristics you can list for isopods and meal worms.

Isopods (Sow Bugs)	Mealworms
_____	_____
_____	_____
_____	_____
_____	_____
_____	_____

2. How can you find out what meal worms and isopods use for food?

   _____

   _____

3. What did you discover about the meal worm's eating habits?

   _____

   _____

4. Where can you find isopods? What do you think isopods eat?

   _____

   _____

5. How do you think meal worms and isopods fit into God's plan and purpose for everything?

   _____

   _____

   _____

   _____

6. Sometimes we feel like no one loves us. In Psalm 22:6, when David was feeling low, he compared himself to a worm: "I am a worm, and no man; a reproach of men, and despised of the people." David poured out his heart to God and by the end of Psalm 22, he begins to praise God because God is his only comfort. What does this show you about the attributes of God?

   a. God loves me when I think no one else does.

   b. _____

   c. _____

> You will have to observe this experiment periodically to notice any progress. You will be setting up containers that you can observe at different times. You will also be observing **decay** and **decomposition**.

I. Decomposers in God's Creation

1. In your own words, what is a decomposer?

   _____
   _____
   _____
   _____
   _____

2. Can you name at least four decomposers?

   a. _____

   b. _____

   c. _____

   d. _____

3. After a while (one week ± a few days), state the results of your decomposition experiment. Were there any differences in the plant, animal, and sand only containers? How long before you observed any evidence of decomposers? Explain your results so far in the space below.

   _____
   _____
   _____
   _____
   _____

4. Can you describe the food web chart below? What types of organisms are in each box?

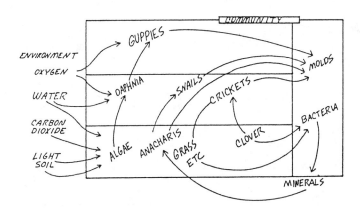 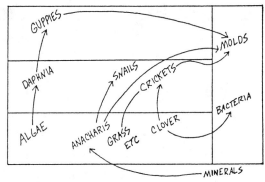

_____

_____

_____

5. What do you think would happen if we didn't have decomposers on the earth? Give your own ideas.

_____

_____

_____

6. What does this lesson on decomposers indicate about the attributes of God?

   a. God had an overall plan for all of His creation.

   b. _____

   c. _____

95

> This will give you an opportunity to see how yeast (a decomposer) will affect food, such as a banana. If you have a good hand lens, you might be able to see some interesting things.

J. Observing Yeast In God's Creation

1. In your own words, what is yeast? You might want to do some library research on yeast.

   _____

   _____

   _____

2. Use the following data chart to record brief observations about your yeast experiment.

DATA CHART FOR: _____		
BANANA & YEAST (WRITE BRIEFLY)	DATE	BANANA W/O YEAST (WRITE BRIEFLY)

3. Are there yeasts in the air? How could you experiment to find this out? (Once again, you may be able to find out many interesting things about yeasts in library books.)

   _____

   _____

   _____

4. Can you think of some other organisms that behave like yeast? Name as many as you can think of here:

   _____   _____

   _____   _____

   _____

5. What do these organisms do in the natural environment? (Hint: If we were to take a walk outside, we would find them in and around rotting logs. See how many you can find in this environment.)

   _____

   _____

6. Can you think of the name for these organisms?

   _____

7. Fill in the food web chart below with the name of one organism (or several organisms) that would fit in each rectangle to complete a food web that occurs in nature. This is going to take some extra research on your part. Get your biology resources out of the library.

FOOD WEB CHART

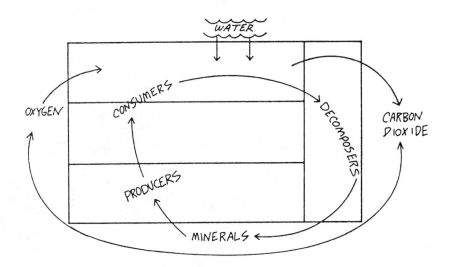

97

8. Can you find out how yeast is used in making bread and explain the process on the lines below? Perhaps you and your mom can get together and bake a loaf of bread to find this out.

   _____

   _____

   _____

   _____

   _____

9. What is **leaven**? (Look this word up in the dictionary if you don't know.)

   _____

   _____

   _____

10. In I Corinthians, Chapter 5 (look this up), the Apostle Paul talks about leaven which symbolizes sin in the Bible. Just as a little yeast can make a huge lump of dough rise, so can a little bit of sin cause many problems in the body of Christ. God uses many illustrations from the world around us to explain spiritual truths. What does this show you about the attributes of God?

    a. God wants us to really understand His ways.

    b. _____

    c. _____

> This is the time for us to see how much you really understand about living communities. Any library research you can do on this subject will help you greatly.

K. Summing up Communities in God's Creation

1. See if you can give an explanation, in your own words, for a **community**.

   _____

   _____

   _____

   _____

   _____

   _____

2. What are some **environmental factors** that cause a community to grow?

   _____   _____

   _____   _____

   _____   _____

3. Can you draw the stages in the reproduction cycle of some organism you observed? (Don't forget to label each step in the cycle.)

4. Draw a line to match the word on the left with the best description on the right.

   Consumer   Returns minerals and nutrients to the soil

   Environmental factor Makes its own food

   Decomposer   Eats green plants

   Producer   Plants, animals and other organisms (bacteria, yeasts) that provide food for other animals

5. Genesis 2:15 tells us that God put Adam in the Garden to dress and keep it. Can you think of three ways that people today "dress and keep" our environment?

   _____

   _____

   _____

6. God gave us the responsibility to take care of the world he has given us. What does this show you about the attributes of God?

   a. God has given man the intelligence to take care of our world.

   b. _____

   c. _____

100

CHAPTER 5

LEVEL F: PHYSICAL SCIENCE

Electric and Magnetic Models in God's Creation

This section on electricity and magnetism will help you to understand much about the secrets of electricity. When you are doing these experiments, you should be aware that there are many things that can go wrong when you are working with electricity. For example, your cell could be dead or run down so that you won't be able to do your experiment, or you may have forgotten to clean a wire of all insulation so your experiment won't work. Keep your eyes open for these things, and have fun with your electricity experiments.

A. Electric and Magnetic Models in God's Creation

1. Take some time to review the vocabulary words that we covered in the teacher's manual. Try your memory on the following:

    System _____

    _____

    _____

    _____

    Subsystem _____

    _____

    _____

    _____

    Interaction _____

    _____

    _____

    _____

    Interaction at a distance _____

    _____

    _____

    _____

Objects _____

_____

_____

_____

_____

Properties

_____

_____

_____

_____

Energy sources

_____

_____

_____

_____

2. We can't see electric currents or magnetic fields, but we know they exist and we will be working with models to show some of their properties. Explain, in your own words, how you know that electricity exists.

_____

_____

_____

3. Let's use the Bible as an example for a model. The Bible tells us that God is three beings in one; God the Father, God the Son (Jesus), and God the Holy Spirit. Here is a model of how they work together.

   a. God is the energy source for the light. _____

   b. _____

   c. _____

This series of experiments will demonstrate how evidence of interaction gives us a clue to the whole idea of magnetism and electricity.

B. Electricity and Magnetism in God's Creation

1. We will be using the word **circuit** frequently. Get your dictionary, and record what it says about an electrical circuit.

   _____

   _____

2. Make a **circuit** like the example below with a switch that will "open" and "close" quickly. Experiment with this system by using your compass.

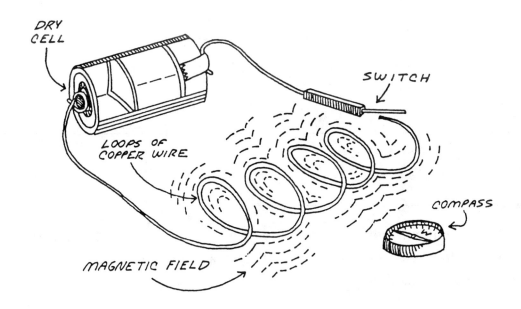

3. Can you tell what the evidence of **magnetic interaction** was in this system? When did it occur?

   _____

   _____

   _____

4. Try each of the following systems with your own batteries, bulb, and wires. When you complete this experiment, tell if it is an **open** or **closed circuit**. Write about this in the space below.

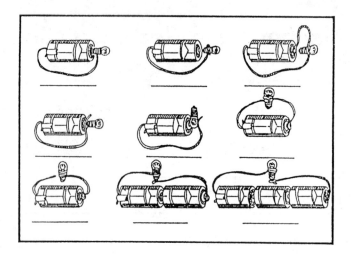

INFERENCE CHART
FOR ELECTRICAL
INTERACTING
SUBSYSTEMS

_____
_____
_____

5. What was the evidence for **electrical interaction** in the systems above? Can you explain when it occurred?

_____
_____
_____

6. Let's experiment with different kinds of wire and other objects to see how effective they are at closing a circuit. Check the box that represents the electrical interaction for each item.

OBJECT TESTED	EXCELLENT	GOOD	POOR	NOT AT ALL
Copper				
Iron				
Aluminum				
Plastic				
Wood				
Salt Water				

7. Which of the following drawings (#7 & #8) represents a **series circuit** and which represents a **parallel circuit**? Explain this, in your own, words in the space below each drawing.

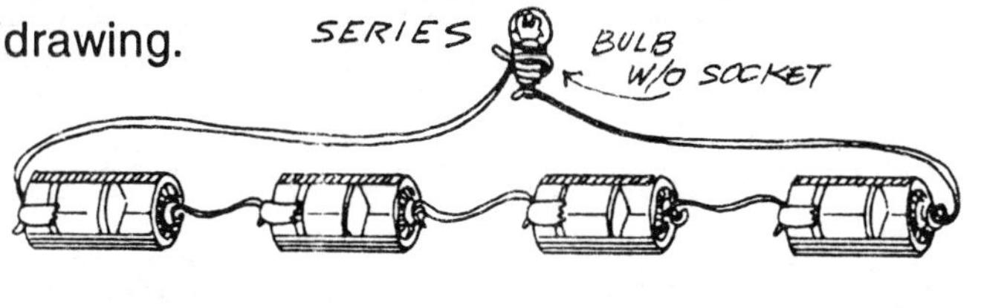

SERIES — BULB W/O SOCKET

_____

8. Which of these **circuits** do you think would be brighter? Can you give a reason for this?

PARALLEL — BULB W/O SOCKET

_____

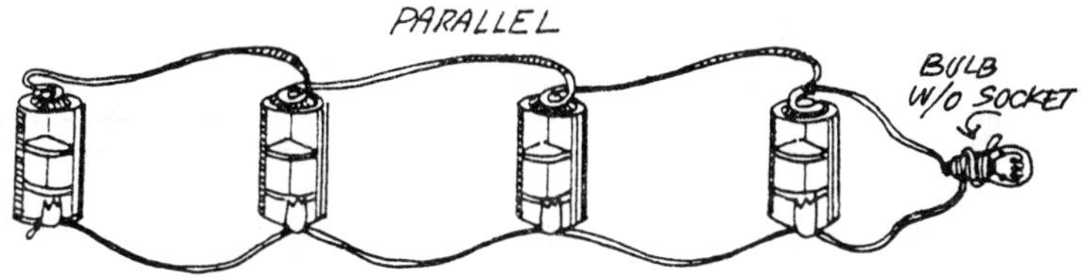

9. Which do you think would last longer? Can you give a reason for this?

_____

_____

10. Test your predictions for each **circuit** with your own battery and bulb. Which one was brighter?

_____

11. Sacrifice two cells by timing how long it takes for them to run down. Record how long it took in each **circuit**.

    parallel _____

    series _____

12. What are some of the variables which could have affected this experiment?

_____

_____

13. God, in all His great wisdom, gave us the use of forces beyond our understanding. What does this show you about the attributes of God?

    a. God is omnipotent (all powerful).

    b. _____

    c. _____

107

> These experiments will make you think hard. You will see electricity produced in very strange ways. The big thinking comes when you are asked to figure out **why**.

C. Examining Models for Energy Sources in God's Creation

1. Do you remember what the difference was between an open and a closed circuit? Explain this in your own words.

   _____
   _____
   _____

2. Notice the cut-in-half dry cell battery below. Explain how you think this might produce electricity. Write your ideas in the blanks below.

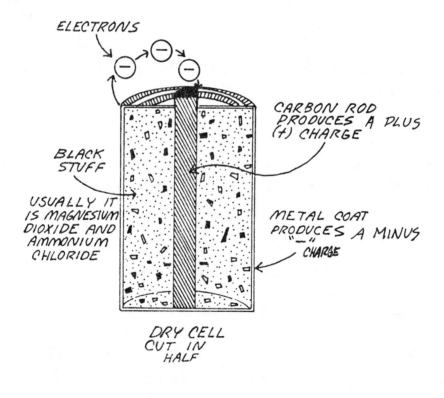

   _____
   _____
   _____
   _____

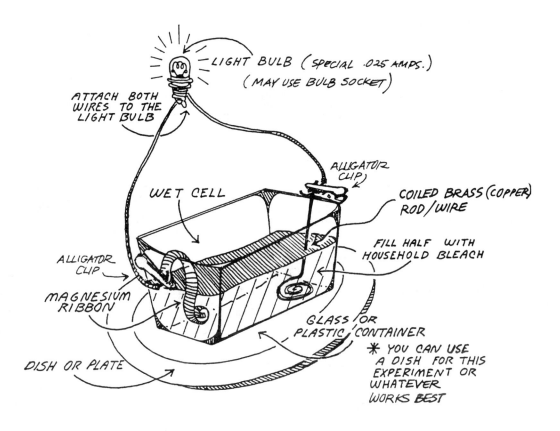

3. In your experiment with the **wet cell**, which end produces the negative (-) charge and which end produces the positive (+) charge? Look at your dry cell and see if this gives you a clue.

_____

_____

_____

4. Try a variety of metal rods, **always using the magnesium ribbon for one terminal**, and see what combination of metals lights the light best. Circle your results below:

magnesium and _____	no light	dim light	bright light
magnesium and _____	no light	dim light	bright light
magnesium and _____	no light	dim light	bright light
magnesium and _____	no light	dim light	bright light

5. In your own words, try to explain what you just observed in the experiments above.

   _____

   _____

   _____

6. What are some of the similarities between a wet and a dry cell?

   _____

   _____

   _____

7. How many subsystems are in the dry cell? _____

8. Can you name them?

   a. _____

   b. _____

   c. _____

   d. _____

   etc. _____

9. How many subsystems are in the wet cell in the drawing above?

   _____

   _____

   _____

10. Can you name them?

    a. _____

    b. _____

    c. _____

    d. _____

    etc. _____

11. What do you think God's purpose was for what we saw in our experiments above? What does this show you about the attributes of God?

    a. God doesn't want us to be lazy about discovering things about Him and His creation.

    b. _____

    c. _____

A model is something that you make up in your own mind or construct with your own hands. Models are only replicas of the real thing. Scientists do not always turn out to be correct. When this happens, the models have to be changed.

D. Working with Models in God's Creation.

(If you have a battery holder for your circuit tester, use it.)

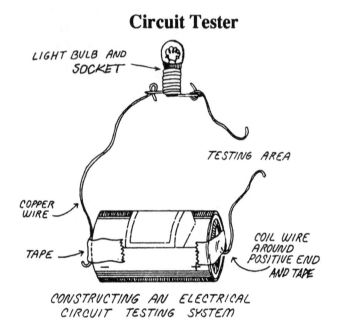

Circuit Tester

CONSTRUCTING AN ELECTRICAL CIRCUIT TESTING SYSTEM

1. Using a circuit tester like the one above, draw a line for each puzzle to show where you found the circuit connected. (Use construction plans in teacher's manual.)

   a.

   b.

   c.

   d.

112

2. Before you open the mystery box, make some predictions about what is inside. List everything you think is inside. (Use plans and directions on V-17 of the teacher's manual.)

_____   _____

_____   _____

_____   _____

_____   _____

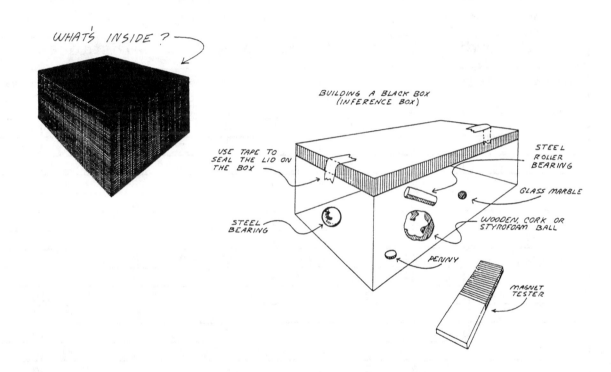

3. Look inside the mystery box and circle each of the items you predicted were in the box.

4. God gave us a brain that is able to think great ideas. These ideas come from what man is able to observe in His creation. What does this show you about the attributes of God?

   a. God has a plan and purpose for man.

   b. _____

   c. _____

> These experiments will give you a real challenge with **magnetic fields**. The harder you think about what is going on, the more you will understand **magnetism**. Great scientists don't completely understand **magnetism**.

E. A Model For a Magnetic Field in God's Creation

1. Experiment with **magnetic attraction** for seven different items (one being a paper clip) at different distances from a **magnet**. List the other six items below "paper clip" on the chart until you have written them each four times, first for the 4" test, second for the 3" test, third for the 2" test, and fourth for the 1" test, then circle the correct number for each object you tried at different distances from the **magnet**.

Recording Magnetic Influence at Various Distances

Object	At 4"	10 = very strong			5 = average			1 = very weak	
Paper Clip	1	2	3	4	5	6	7	8	9	10
	1	2	3	4	5	6	7	8	9	10
	1	2	3	4	5	6	7	8	9	10
	1	2	3	4	5	6	7	8	9	10
	1	2	3	4	5	6	7	8	9	10
	1	2	3	4	5	6	7	8	9	10
	1	2	3	4	5	6	7	8	9	10
At 3"										
Paper Clip	1	2	3	4	5	6	7	8	9	10
	1	2	3	4	5	6	7	8	9	10
	1	2	3	4	5	6	7	8	9	10
	1	2	3	4	5	6	7	8	9	10
	1	2	3	4	5	6	7	8	9	10
	1	2	3	4	5	6	7	8	9	10
	1	2	3	4	5	6	7	8	9	10
At 2"										
Paper Clip	1	2	3	4	5	6	7	8	9	10
	1	2	3	4	5	6	7	8	9	10
	1	2	3	4	5	6	7	8	9	10
	1	2	3	4	5	6	7	8	9	10
	1	2	3	4	5	6	7	8	9	10
	1	2	3	4	5	6	7	8	9	10
	1	2	3	4	5	6	7	8	9	10
At 1"										
Paper Clip	1	2	3	4	5	6	7	8	9	10
	1	2	3	4	5	6	7	8	9	10
	1	2	3	4	5	6	7	8	9	10
	1	2	3	4	5	6	7	8	9	10
	1	2	3	4	5	6	7	8	9	10
	1	2	3	4	5	6	7	8	9	10
	1	2	3	4	5	6	7	8	9	10

2. Create the electromagnet below by placing a loop of coated copper wire in an electrical circuit with a dry cell battery.

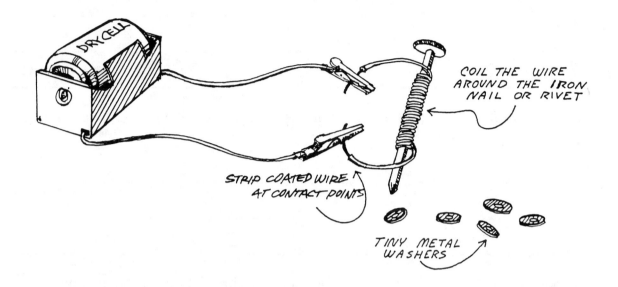

3. What happens when you "complete" (or "close") the circuit?

_____
_____
_____
_____

4. What happens when you "open" the circuit?

_____
_____
_____
_____

5. List the subsystems in this experiment.

_____
_____
_____
_____

6. Experiment with two magnets to help discover if both ends of a magnet have the same properties. Explain your results here.

   _____
   _____
   _____

7. Experiment with a magnet and a compass. How does this help to build a model for a magnetic field?

   _____
   _____
   _____

8. Magnetism and magnetic fields are phenomena that defy a perfect scientific explanation. Man has studied these forces through the ages and has learned how to use them, but the cause of the forces eludes him. What does this show you about the attributes of God?

   a. God works in many ways that we cannot understand.

   b. _____

   c. _____

9. Make an electromagnet like the following drawing, with three turns of wire around the nail, and "close" the circuit. How many washers were picked up? Record your results by making a point on the following graph, and continue to record the number of turns and effect on washers on the data graph.

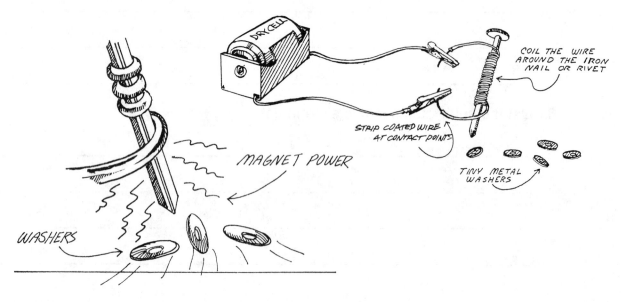

116

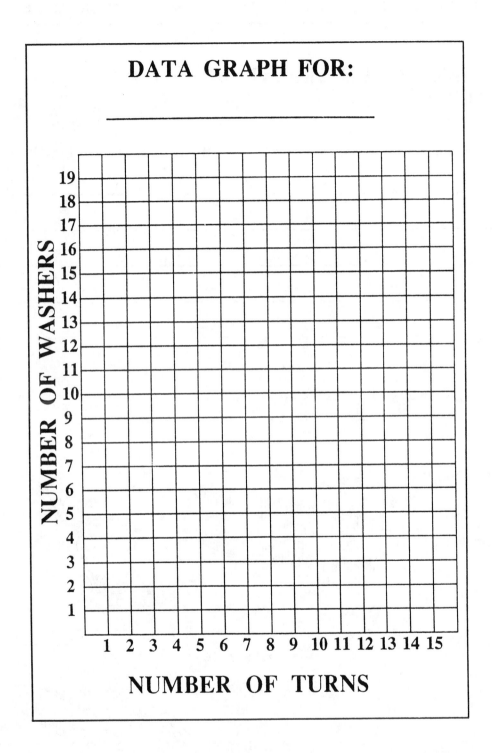

This lesson will help you to see a clear spiritual principle in a simple scientific experiment with magnets. Try your best to think this experiment through carefully.

F. Broken Magnet/Broken Relationships in God's Creation

1. Write a paragraph to explain your broken magnet experiment in detail.

   _____
   _____
   _____
   _____
   _____

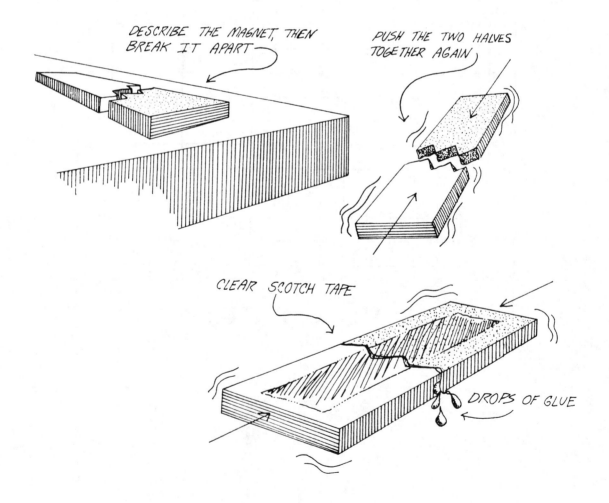

2. Has the tape or glue "healed" the broken parts permanently? Explain this.

   _____

   _____

   _____

3. The only thing that can heal the sin-caused broken relationship between the sinner and God is for us to believe in the Person and work of our Redeemer, Jesus Christ (Galatians 2:16). By sacrificing Himself on the cross, His shed blood provides a covering for our sins, and His broken body provides for complete healing (Isaiah 53:5).

4. What does this show you about the attributes of God?

   a. God can heal my broken relationships if I believe in the work He sent Jesus to do for me.

   b. _____

   c. _____

> Just as we can discover invisible magnetic fields by studying magnets, so also we can discover some of God's invisible qualities by studying His creation.

G. Seeing the Invisible become Visible in God's Creation (Romans 1:20)

1. Place two magnets on edge, opposite poles facing one another and far enough apart so that they won't attract one another. Carefully place one-half sheet of a manila folder over the two magnets. Sprinkle iron filings over the magnets. Write a short paragraph to explain your observations.

   _____
   _____
   _____
   _____
   _____
   _____

2. "For the invisible things of Him from the creation of the world are clearly seen, being understood by the things that are made, even His eternal power and Godhead; so that they are without excuse" (Romans 1:20).

   Underline the two invisible attributes of God that we can see from the things that He has made in this world.

3. What are some other words you can think of that mean "power"?

   _____
   _____
   _____
   _____
   _____

4. People often have a worldly nature (selfish, lazy, mean, wicked, self-serving, back-biting, etc.), but we often see examples of a divine (heavenly) nature here on earth. List several examples of a divine nature. For example: caring and forgiving.

   _____   _____

   _____   _____

   _____   _____

   _____   _____

5. What is the most impressive man-made thing you have ever seen?

   _____

   _____

6. What do you think about the person who made or designed it?

   _____

   _____

7. What is the most impressive thing that you have ever seen in God's creation?

   _____

   _____

8. What does this show you about the attributes (divine nature or power) of God?

   a. God is very intelligent.

   b. _____

   c. _____

CHAPTER 6

LEVEL F: LIFE SCIENCE

Ecosystems in God's Creation

> This section is for the teacher to read in order to create some instructional guidelines; however, it is also within the framework of study for the self-motivated student. After reading, go to Section B.

A. Ecosystems in God's Creation

Ecosystems cover a wide range of learning activities. The instruction surrounding ecosystems will include the life-science concepts previously studied from the first year to the present. Your pupils will investigate the exchange of matter and energy between organisms and their environment and will learn that there must be a continuous balance in the "ecosystem." Whenever there is a change or variation in the system, such as the elimination of an organism through pollution or the destruction of a habitat, it could become harmful to the other organisms. In this series of activities, pupils are asked to constantly evaluate the interactions in the ecosystem. These interactions include exchange of gases, cycling of materials, etc., between organisms and the environment. This concept is perhaps the single most-important concept with which pupils can be confronted in science. It deals directly with the world in which they live and, of course, ultimately with the plan and purpose of God's creation.

The activities in this study are generally slow moving and often subtle in nature; nevertheless, you will find that there are peak times when classroom attention can intensify. You may find that some organisms are hard to catch in quantity, such as crickets, but the challenge for pupils to do the collecting will usually produce an adequate supply. If not, you might want to use mealworms. In other words, there is no specific kind of organism to use. The questioning techniques used in these various activities are vital. If your pupils are going to develop an operational understanding of the process skills of scientific inquiry, they must experience them. Always keep God's plan and purpose before the pupils. They will find the beauty of organisms, interacting in a variety of ways, to be a great testimony to our Creator.

> You will be constructing an ecosystem of your own in these experiments. You may have to start this ecosystem several times before it gets going nicely. See what you can find out about the interaction of organisms when you get this completed.

B. Classroom Ecosystems in God's Creation

1. Build your terrarium/aquarium system according to the drawing below. You may wish to modify this with your own plans. Pay particular attention to the cut-away drawing for making a bridge with soda straws.

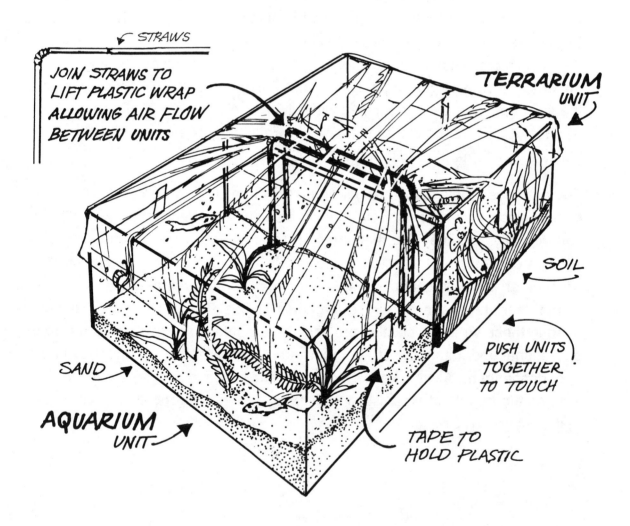

> Before you add crickets to the ecosystem, take some time to study all you can about crickets from library information. You will be surprised what you will learn.

C. Adding Crickets and Guppies to the Ecosystem in God's Creation

(Read about cautions with overcrowding crickets.)

1. Make an observation and inference chart for observing of your ecosystem on a daily basis. Use the drawing below for a guideline.

POPULATION NAME	YOUR INFERENCE AS TO WHY THE CHANGE OCCURRED

2. Make a food pyramid out of the organisms in their ecosystem. Use the drawing below for a guideline.

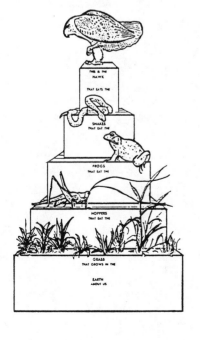
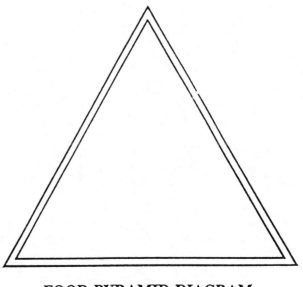

FOOD PYRAMID DIAGRAM

3. What attribute of God might fit into what you have learned about crickets?

   a. God holds on to us firmly.

   b. _____

   c. _____

> This segment will require very careful observation on your part. Some of the changes that occur will be very slight. Keep your eyes open and record everything you see.

D. Changes in the Aquarium and Terrarium Ecosystems in God's Creation

1. Keep a chart similar to the one below to record your daily observations.

DATA CHART			
ORGANISMS	OBSERVATION DATE	CHANGES	CAUSES AND INFERENCE

2. See if you can detect a new organism forming in your ecosystem. Describe this organism in your own words. If it looks something like the drawing below, it might be a mold. (This would be magnified many hundreds of times.)

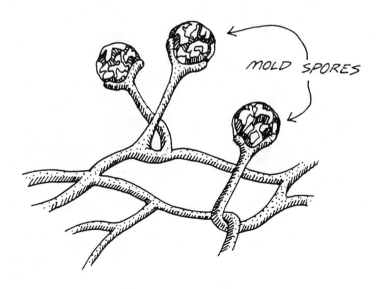

3. Can you think of an attribute of God that will fit into these observations?

   a. The Holy Spirit can't be clearly seen by us, but when you give Him time to develop in your heart and mind, then everyone notices the change in you.

   b. _____

   c. _____

An ecosystem has all the parts that we have been studying put together. It is the air we breath, the ground we walk on, the soil we plant seeds in, the clouds, the rain, and everything about us. The ecosystem is the place where animals and man survive. The earth is a huge ecosystem, the city you live in is a smaller ecosystem, and the microscopic drop of water is the ecosystem for the bacteria and the single-celled algae. You will be asked many questions about the ecosystem in this section.

E. Developing the Concept of an Ecosystem in God's Creation

1. Using the paragraph above, what can you say about your aquarium/terrarium ecosystem?

2. Using the paragraph above, what organisms could survive in your ecosystem?

3. Develop a community chart similar to the one below for your aquarium/terrarium ecosystem.

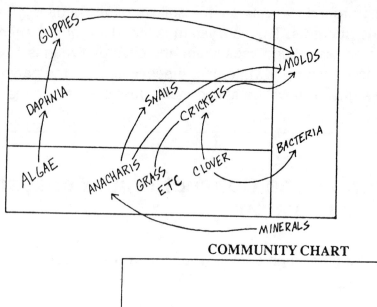

COMMUNITY CHART

4. Add imaginary environmental factors such as rain, sunshine, etc., to your ecosystem and predict what will happen. Record these factors on a chart like the one below.

ENVIRONMENTAL FACTOR	ORGANISM	EFFECTS OF CHANGE

5. From your observations of your ecosystem on a daily basis, fill out the chart below.

ENVIRONMENTAL	EFFECTS OF CHANGE
(EXAMPLE) TEMPERATURE INCREASED TO 79°	ORGANISMS (CRICKET) SEEMED TO BE MORE ACTIVE
1.	
2.	
3.	
4.	
5.	
6.	
7.	
8.	
9.	

6. Looking at the observations you have made of your ecosystem, how does God fit into this picture?

   a. God planned every step of this fragile ecosystem when He created the earth.

   b. _____

   c. _____

133

> Once again, you will be asked to do extensive observations in your ecosystem and outside of your ecosystem. Make sure that you notice everything that happens so you can **infer** what the cause is.

F. Investigating the Water Cycle in God's Creation

1. State your own explanation of what a water cycle is:

   _____
   _____
   _____

2. Keeping the water cycle in mind, add the following experimental ideas, and record your results.

   a. Construct an experiment with a plastic cover over your terrarium/aquarium.

   b. Put some tiny organism, such as a sow bug, or cricket, in a small, air-tight container for awhile. Observe the container carefully. Record your results.

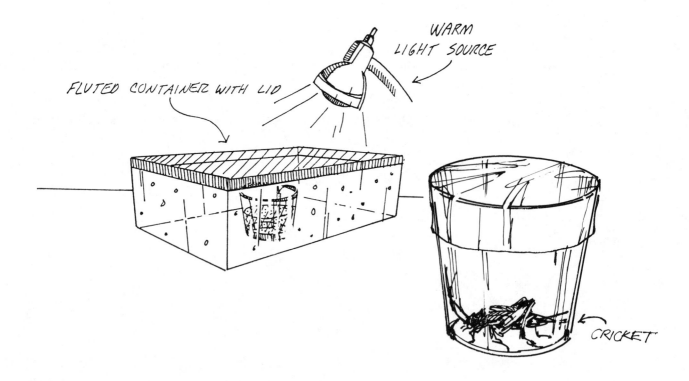

3. Construct an experiment with a pea plant or some other plant that grows quickly and has green leaves. Let the plant grow to maturity and then set it up according to the directions on Page IV-20 of the manual. After you have observed the plant for several days, see if you can answer some of the following questions.

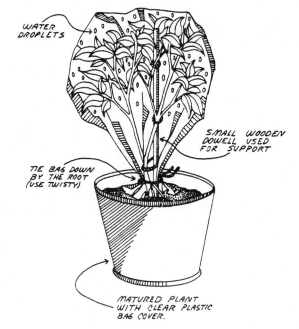

E.

4. What are your general observations?

_____
_____
_____
_____

5. Where is the moisture source in all three experiments?

    a. In the terrarium/aquarium study?

    _____

    b. In the animal organism study?

    _____

    c. In the plant study?

    _____

6. Can you think of an idea for an experiment that will help you to become more certain of your ideas? Try your idea for an experiment:

_____
_____

7. Add heat and light to your experiment and observe the effect that this has on the organism.

_____

_____

_____

_____

8. Pour ice water into a vial or tumbler and observe the results of this experiment.

_____

_____

_____

9. See if you can summarize everything you have done in these experiments in one paragraph. Think how the cricket, the sow bug, the plant, and the ice cube experiments turned out.

_____

_____

_____

10. Think of an attribute of God that might fit into this experiment.

   a. <u>God created a perfect system for the survival of all of His creation.</u>

   b. _____

   c. _____

> You will be using the interesting chemical BTB to help discover some things about gases in this experiment.

G. Experimenting with BTB in God's Creation

1. Let's try the experiment that you did in Level B with BTB again, just for practice.

   Fill your beaker about 1/2 full of tap water, and add enough BTB to make it blue enough so you can clearly see the blue color. Blow into it with a soda straw and observe the color change (see Book I, Page IV-21).

   a. State, in your own words, what caused the color change.

   _____

   _____

   b. Do you have any ideas for an experiment that would test your theory to see if it is true?

   _____

   _____

   c. Can you think of a **variable** that you can control, and find out why sometimes we see **green** colors and sometimes **yellow**? _____

   d. Experiment with vinegar, ammonia, and dry ice to see if you can find more clues to the BTB mystery.

   Vinegar _____

   Ammonia _____

   Dry ice _____

2. Experiment with BTB solutions in the air.
   a. Set open beaker in room for one hour, and observe.
   b. Set open beaker in room for one day, and observe.
   c. Set open beaker in room overnight, and observe.
   d. What conclusions can you come to after you have done a, b, and c?

   _____

   _____

3. What happens to the BTB solution when you run a tube from a vial containing two seltzer tablets into the BTB? Set up your experiment like the one below:

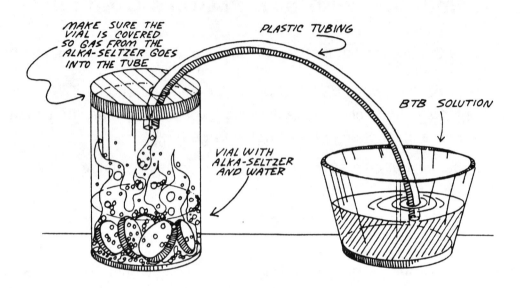

a. State your observations.

_____

_____

_____

b. What do you think caused this to happen?

_____

_____

_____

4. Try this experiment and see if it gives you more information about the BTB question.

   a. Place BTB into a bottle of 7-Up drink.

   b. Seal the top of the bottle firmly.

   c. Place a plastic bag tightly over the top of the BTB solution and run the tube into it.

d. Set your experiment up like the one in the drawing below. This experiment may take as long as two days to change.

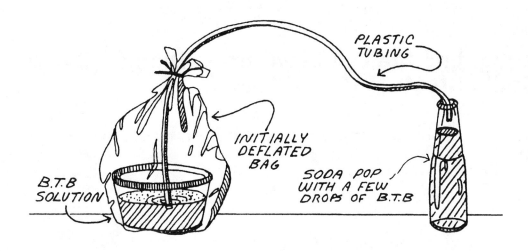

5. See if you can answer some simple questions about your observations:

   a. What caused the interaction?

   _____

   b. What evidence of interaction did you see?

   _____

   c. State your observations.

   _____

6. What attributes of God could you fit into this series of experiments?

   a. <u>God gives us the intellect to follow simple clues and find answers.</u>

   b. _____

   c. _____

One of the very important cycles in any ecosystem is called the oxygen/carbon dioxide cycle. You will be doing some neat experiments to help you gain information about this.

H. Investigating the Oxygen/Carbon Dioxide Cycle in God's Creation

1. Study the chart below for a few minutes and see if you can answer Questions 2 and 3.

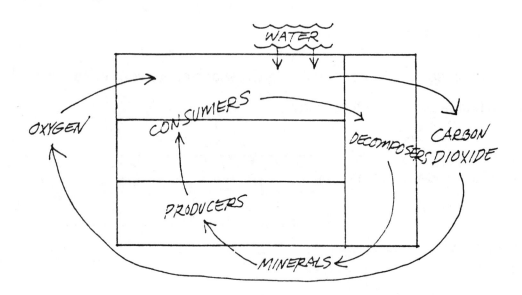

2. Explain, in your own words, how **carbon dioxide** fits into the ecosystem gas cycle.

_____

_____

_____

_____

3. Explain, in your own words, how **oxygen** fits into the ecosystem gas cycle.

_____

_____

_____

_____

4. Set up the following experiment just like the drawings below and answer Questions 5, 6, and 7. Place a small amount of elodea with a few drops of BTB into the vial and cap the vial. Cap the control vial also, but without the elodea. Place a snail into another vial and cap it, also. Cap the control vial, but without the snail.

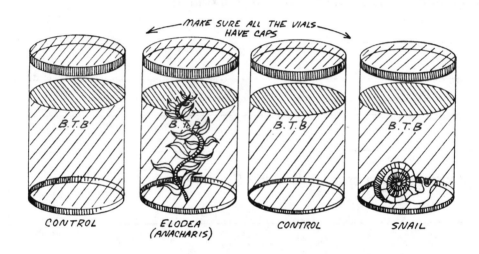

5. Set up a data chart like the one below.

DATA CHART			
	BLUE	GREEN	YELLOW
SNAIL AND B.T.B.			
CONTROL B.T.B.			
ELODEA OR ANACHARIS (+) B.T.B.			
CONTROL (+) B.T.B.			

141

6. Everyone who is around the experiment should make a data chart so that everyone can pool their data at the end of the experiment.

7. You might try an experiment with dark and light for the elodea and the snail. Don't forget to take your control with you. What did you observe?

8. Do animals produce carbon dioxide? Explain.

9. Do plants produce carbon dioxide? Explain.

10. Explain how plants might use carbon dioxide.

11. Look at the drawing below and see if you can explain how the carbon dioxide and oxygen cycle might work.

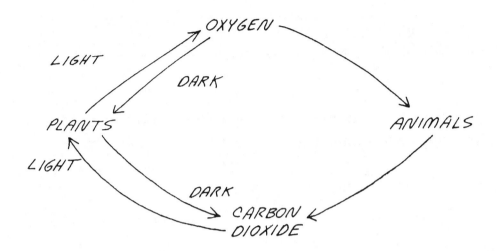

12. The carbon dioxide gas molecule is shaped something like the drawing below. Can you tell why it is written CO_2?

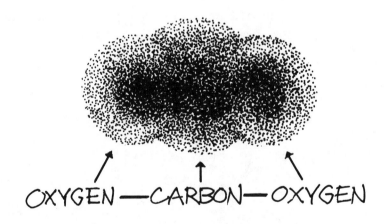

_____
_____
_____
_____

13. Explain, in your own words, what you observed about the gases coming from the elodea plant and the snail.

   _____
   _____
   _____
   _____

14. Explain, in your own words, what happened when you placed the plant in the dark? Compare this with the plant that was kept in the light.

   _____
   _____
   _____
   _____

15. Set up as many experiments as you can think of to test the plant and animal gases with BTB. Make sure that you have a control for your experiments, and that you record your results carefully.

16. Set up an experiment like the one below using a pea plant or a plant called a coleus. Place your plants in a dark, light, or even a dimly-lit place. Observe the plant carefully.

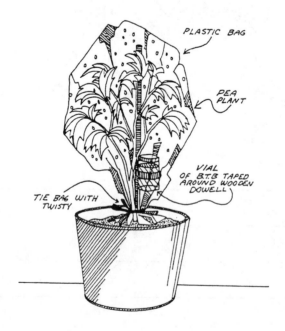

17. Think about how the Creator fits into the whole idea of gas cycles in plants and animals. See if you can come up with some ideas.

   a. God, the Creator, has an orderly and very complete pattern for all of His creation.

   b. _____

   c. _____

You will be putting together everything that you have experimented with in this section. Let's see how much you can get into an ecosystem. You will have to think hard about this section.

I. Cycles in an Ecosystem in God's Creation

1. Think about all of the cycles you can imagine in an ecosystem. Mineral cycles, producer cycles, consumer cycles, decomposer cycles, gas cycles, water cycles, etc. Now place these into a master ecosystem with the producers on the bottom and the consumers in their various pyramid levels at the top. Don't forget the gases and decomposers on the sides. Make your master ecosystem something like the model on page 140.

    Ecosystem

    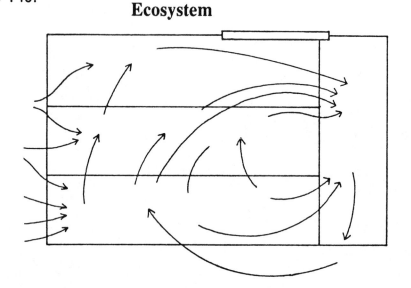

    1. ALGAE
    2. ANACHARIS
    3. BACTERIA
    4. CARBON DIOXIDE
    5. CLOVER
    6. CRICKETS
    7. DAPHNIA
    8. ENVIRONMENT
    9. GRASS
    10. GUPPIES
    11. LIGHT SOIL
    12. MINERALS
    13. MOLDS
    14. OXYGEN
    15. SNAILS
    16. WATER

2. Write a paragraph on everything you can think of regarding your ecosystem food web chart.

    _____
    _____
    _____
    _____
    _____
    _____

3. Can you think of an attribute of God that the Creator had in mind, when He placed all of these cycles in place at the time of creation?

   a. God had perfection in mind when He set out to do His creation.

   b.

   c.